WHEN THOU PASSEST THROUGH THE WATERS

by

Josephine Fitzgerald

"Must Reading For Mending Broken Hearts"

**A Doorkeeper Gift
J. Gordon Henry Ministries
2114 Arrow Court
Murfreesboro, TN 37130
(6159 890-8384 or 890-6264**

Copyright © by Josephine Fitzgerald, June 1990

All rights reserved.

Cover design by Rev. Ron Sathe

Royalty Publishing Co.
P.O. Box 2016
Manassas, VA 22110

Library of Congress Number 90-60867

ISBN 0-910487-21-9

DEDICATION

This book is dedicated to a real servant of the Lord, Gladys Billings, without who's faithful witness this could not have been written.

HELP FOR THE HURTING

There is so much heartache around these days. Please pray that my book will get into the hands of hurting people.

If you can help with cost of production please send what you can. No one will be refused if they cannot afford to give anything.

Write to: Josephine Fitzgerald
   Rt. 1, Box 56
   Lovingston, VA 22949

FOREWORD

How does God build a person's character? Are we willing to recognize the guiding hand of the Lord as we find in this account?

Herein is a wondrous life being built through mistakes and trials, through prayers and praise. Not many in life will confess their weaknesses and their blessings as this lovable grandmother. Identify yourself with her touching moments of great trial; her simple faith and seeking a solution through humanly trust, leaning on a wisdom only known by those who walk by faith. See her now, in the sunset of life, full of grace and kindness, loved by all her children and grandchildren.

Josephine's son-in-law,
Rev. Norbert G. Prust

Some Thru the Waters
Some Thru the Flood
Some Thru the Fire
But All Thru the Blood;
Some Thru Great Sorrow
But God Gives a Song
In the Night Season
And All the Day Long.

Through the weeks preceding the wreck the Lord kept before me that verse, "THAT I MAY KNOW HIM AND THE POWER OF HIS RESURRECTION AND THE FELLOWSHIP OF HIS SUFFERING AND BE MADE CONFORMABLE UNTO HIS DEATH." I would ponder over that verse and always remark, "If we want the power, we must be willing to suffer." I knew that I wanted the power, not to hold over others, but that His word would be spoken with such power that it would reach out to souls who would yield to the Lord.

I have had the joy of following the Lord for forty some odd years, through heartache, trials and mistakes. I will try to tell it like it was. Many times the things I went through show me in a very bad light, but even these reveal the patience and the love of our Lord.

I have found out one thing, if we really want the Lord to have first place in our lives, He will use any one or anything we put before Him to refine us, to take away the shallow things, to heed His call; "Come up a little higher." Never should we condemn the instrument that God uses, but seek to live in such a way that it will be used of God to win the other person, as well as refine us.

Whatever or whomever we put before the Lord is our idol and must be revealed to us in their true light. Little by little the Lord will lead us in such a way that they lose their hold on us.

One experiences many lessons, and much needed pruning from our Lord.

May He continue to prune me as long as I am on this earth.

                        Mary Josephine Fitzgerald

ACKNOWLEDGEMENTS

Just how do you go about thanking all the precious ones that had a part in completing this book. I want you all to know that it has been a great joy to work together with you.

I owe special thanks to:

Elaine Prust and Cathy Monnin, my granddaughters, for the insurmountable task of committing my scribbling into a typewritten text.

Betty-Jo Prust, my daughter, for taking a lot of pages and organizing them into a book with chapter divisions. She even gave titles to some of the chapters.

Nita Scoggans, a publisher, for helping me to refine the form and organization of the book.

Brenda Fitzgerald, my daughter-in-law, for her helpful suggestions.

Mary Ann Sathe, my pastor's wife, for helping me to tell of my experiences in a way which would help readers to understand it better. I have affectionately called her "My Editor".

Rev. Ron Sathe for design of the cover.

The precious one who did not want her name mentioned for helping to correct the grammar.

Last but not least, I extend my appreciation to Faye Bailey, a precious friend of mine, and her friend, Elaine Ross, who have done the final typing and corrections.

Again I say thanks! Without all of you, I could not have done it. Above all, I thank my God for the guiding and helping hand of the Holy Spirit by the love of Jesus Christ.

Josephine Fitzgerald

Broken Dreams

*As children bring
their broken toys
With tears for us to mend.
I brought my broken dreams
to God
Because He was my Friend.*

*But then instead
of leaving Him
In peace to work alone,
I hung around
and tried to help
With ways
that were my own.*

*At last I snatched them back
and cried,
"How can You be so slow"—
"My child," He said,
"What could I do?
You never did let go."*

    Author Unknown

TABLE OF CONTENTS

DEDICATION III
FOREWORD # 1 IV
FOREWORD # 2 V
ACKNOWLEDGEMENT VI
BROKEN DREAMS VII

CHAPTERS	PAGE
1. God's Miraculous Protection	1
2. Childhood Memories, Training and Early Marriage	5
3. God's Drawing to Salvation and Overcoming Temptation	10
4. Surrendering My Will for His	16
5. The Lord Speaks to Me about Being in Debt	20
6. How the Lord Led in the Tithe	24
7. Enduring Temptation	26
8. God Gives Strength and Wisdom and Continues to Answer Prayer	30
9. The Keeping Hand of the Lord	34
10. God's Grace In Our Lives	41
11. Following on to Walk with the Lord	45
12. Can God?	53
13. God's Providence and Man's Frailty	58
14. Trust and Obey	63
15. Miracles of the Lord	72
16. God's Plan and Purpose	76
17. I Will Never Leave Thee	82
18. God's Love Drives Out Fear	88
19. Let Him Have His Way with Thee	91
20. God's Appropriate Time	98
21. Watching God Work	107
22. God Leads Us Along	111
BIBLIOGRAPHY	114

CHAPTER ONE

God's Miraculous Protection

"When thou passest through the waters, I will be with thee; and through the rivers, they shall not overflow thee: when thou walketh through the fire, thou shalt not be burned; neither shall the flame kindle upon thee." Isaiah 43:2

Spring of 1986 is here, and this week has been lovely. The weather is warm, and what a joy it is to go into the yard and see the flowers and the fruit trees in bloom. At this point it is a picture of beauty. Everywhere I look, I am reminded of the resurrection story. As I let my thoughts wander back over this past year, it has been one that has both joy and sorrow, — one of those full years. This is the first week of April. Last year at this time life was going along normally for me. I had a '73 red Pinto which I drove to church, grocery shopping, etc. It was old, but so was I. We got along well, even though I was always having to put it in the shop. One day in May my children had me come to Richmond, and there they presented me with a 1984 Chevette. The joy of getting behind that wheel after the Pinto was wonderful. I drove home on cloud nine.

I kept my grandchildren that summer, and since they loved books, when things got rough, I would pile them into the car, and we would go to the library. It surely made a difference.

At that time, I began keeping my grandchildren one at a time. Sometimes I was even brave enough to keep all three on Wednesday and Sunday nights, so I could take them to church. I had "little church" for the children on those nights. Later, when they went to Atlanta, I went with them for ten days. Then I came back on the train, because I had some guests coming. The highlight of that trip was stopping in Charlotte, N.C. to see Glad, the precious lady who made my Lord so real to me. She was paralyzed then, but what a testimony to the Lord! She was in perfect peace. She could

1

talk, so we talked to each other. I asked her how she would have me pray for her and she said, "Pray that I will always be obedient to my Lord. I have read my Bible through seventy six times." What a testimony! My son Tom had gone out of his way to take me to see her, and this proved to be the last time we had fellowship together. She is now with her Lord in Glory.

I had the joy of having missionaries in my home and what fellowship we had together. The summer just flew by.

The last of August, Stephanie, my youngest granddaughter, and I got in the car and drove into Charlottesville. We went to visit Betty Dunnevant, a good friend of mine, to help her with a moving sale. While we were there, Steve, my pastor, and his family came over to get some things they had left there and I offered to carry them home in my car.

Trici, their 4 year old, wanted to ride with us. So I put the two little girls in the front seat with the seatbelt around them, but I failed to put on mine.

The weather was beautiful that day, and there was very little traffic. We were driving along, when the wheel was jerked out of my hand and into a road sign I went. The sign snapped in two and flipped over the car, turning us just in time to keep us from hitting a stone embankment. The children did not have a scratch on them. The Lord was good! I had to go to the emergency room for stitches where I had real fellowship with a Christian doctor. We talked while he was sewing me up. People came from everywhere to help us. They took the children in hand, gave them drinks, and did what they could for me.

When I had an opportunity to assess what had happened, I understood that there had been a mechanical failure under the car. The left side locked up, and I had no control over the steering of the car. Although my car was demolished, the children were protected. Praise the Lord!

About three weeks later Jeff, my grandson that lived with me, and I were in the yard working with the flowers. To my surprise, Bobby, my second oldest son, came down and took me to Richmond to pick out another car. I picked out a 1984 Dodge Omni and drove it home. It too drove beautifully.

About a week later we were having a revival. Betty and I were having meetings for the children. Emmett, Betty's husband, was preaching. Satan really fought that revival. A virus swept through the church and on Wednesday night I caught it and was sick all night. I slept all day Thursday and didn't intend to go to church that night, but Betty called and said that she was sick and couldn't come, and so I went.

It had been raining that day and was still drizzling. As I started home, I got off on the loose gravel on the side of the road. As I turned the wheel to get back on the road, my wheel hit a bad place on the shoulder. My car went airborne. I went across the road, down a hill and landed upside down, hugging the hill. The car was demolished in such a way that it couldn't be seen from the road.

I had a full tank of gas but there was no fire. As I went over the hill, all the lights went out. I was trapped under the seat. There were pain and chills, but the thing I think of when I look back, was the presence of the Lord. I had such peace, and He gave that lovely verse, "And we know that all things work together for good to them that love God, to them that are the called according to His purpose." And always in the recess of my mind there was a choir singing, and the hymn I heard the most was, "How Great Thou Art", and truly He is great. It seemed as though He held a pillow between me and the pain.

When Jeff got home, he did a super job in sending different people out to search for me. He called the pastor first, then neighbors, and the rescue squad, but it was 14 hours later before they found me. Again, it is unbelievable how wonderful people are. Everybody was concerned. They searched all night until 11:30 the next morning.

When they found me and came down to see about me, I said, "Please help me." They rejoiced to know that I was alive. When they got me to the hospital, the doctors were so nice. I remember one doctor saying this ought to be on T.V. Another one said, "Read all about her in Reader's Digest on page 78." Later, I saw a Reader's Digest in the doctor's office and turned to page 78. The story was of a man that had been miraculously saved from an accident.

I was admitted to the hospital with 6 broken ribs, a broken collarbone, and a punctured lung. I was getting along well, even getting up with the walker, when blood clots were found. I was in the hospital three weeks. All the time I was there, I felt that God took me in His arms and carried me through. The doctors and nurses were super. They would come in some times just to talk, so I was able to give my testimony to several of them.

I got out of the hospital on October 24th and the children took care of me through January 6, 1986. All my children came, and since they were all from different states, they worked out a schedule whereby different ones gave up their vacations and came to care for me. Even an ex-daughter-in-law came from a different state and stayed two weeks with me.

They not only took care of me, but spent so much of their own money. Never have I seen so much love as I saw from my family and friends. While I was in the hospital, neighbors and church members sent in food to feed my loved ones. I received over 100 cards and many flowers. Emmett said that the night after the accident the Spirit of the Lord broke through at the revival. I will never forget the concern of my family and friends for me. Truly, we have a wonderful Lord! Always after an experience like that, we come through loving our Lord a little more.

So now I have seen another spring and I feel wonderfully blessed. I know that God preserved my life.

CHAPTER TWO

Childhood Memories, Training and Early Marriage

I share the memories of my life, to show how God does work to bring about His good purpose and draw us closer to Himself!

My hope is that this book may be a help to someone who is seeking a closer walk with the Lord in the midst of trials and struggles.

Thinking back to my childhood, the earliest memory I have is of our home on Swartz Avenue in Louisville, Kentucky. At that time, I was between the age of four and five.

I had a wonderful mother who was always there, but mostly in the background. Papa was a salesman and was gone most of the time.

As I grew up, my sister Louise and I were very close. We did everything together. I had a younger sister, Catherine, one older brother Anthony and my oldest sister Margaret.

When Louise started to school, they tell me that I would slip over to the school and peep through the windows and try to do what the others did. The school was just around the corner from our house. So, the teachers finally let me come to school before I was of age.

In 1918 right after the war, Papa, who at that time was part owner of a tire company, told Mama that he was moving to Dayton, Ohio, to take over the other store. He told her that we couldn't go, because the blacks went to school with the whites, and he didn't want his kids raised that way. I can remember that Mama cried a lot at night after we were put to bed.

When Papa moved to Dayton, Mama moved us all back to Owensboro, Kentucky to Grandma's house. I didn't realize it at the time, but I was never to see my Father again. We lived with Grandma until I was fourteen. We then moved back to Louisville.

Mama got a job, because at that time Papa was sick and unable to send us any money for support. Near the end of Papa's life,

Mama found out that he had been living with another woman. He died when I was sixteen.

I never felt the lack in not having a daddy. When he was home, there was so much tension, we kids were glad when he left.

Mama was a wonderful Mother. She gave up her life to raise us.

We were raised in a good moral home. We did not have a lot of worldly goods, but we had good Sunday clothes and a couple of good school dresses. I never remember having to worry about whether we would have something to eat or not, because food was always there.

We were raised in the Catholic religion and went to the Catholic school. I have many fond memories there: taking my first communion, being confirmed, and on Christmas getting up at 5 o'clock and dressing, walking often in the snow to go to 5:30 mass, seeing the beautiful manger scene, and on the way home always wondering what Santa Claus brought us.

I remember as a child going to Communion and thinking on the way out, "I have to be good now because God is in me." When I was confirmed I took the name of Teresa, because it meant, "Little flower of Jesus". I saw my Mother on her knees for an hour every night, saying her rosary and always asking the Lord to keep her well, so she could raise us. She never had a life of her own, socially. She never even dated, so that when we were married, she could be free to come to us if we needed her.

I do hope in the years to come, when I am gone, that my children will have good memories of me. My Mother lived to be 89 years old and was always precious. She will be in and out of this writing, because she is so much a part of my life.

My sister Louise had trouble with her eyes, so she was held back, and we went through school together. Everyone thought that we were twins. Mama was always there if we needed her, but unless there was a need, we were too busy playing. We had to do the dishes every night. One week I washed and Louise dried; the next week we reversed. I remember always hiding the oatmeal pan since it was so hard to wash. We had to dust every Saturday and carry in the coal. Other than those chores we were free to play.

I will always remember our dining room table. After supper it was cleaned off, and we five children had to sit around it, doing our homework. On rainy days we played games on it. We loved to read, and walked to the library to get books. Louisa M. Alcott and Gene Stratton Porter, are some of the authors that I remember. We read books such as the *Bobbsey Twin's* Serials, *Camp Fire Girls, Little Women, Ann of Green Gables, The Little Colonel, The Five Little Peppers and How They Grew*, and many of Grace Livingston Hill's books. These were all clean wholesome reading.

When we moved back to Louisville, I had to transfer to public school. Their teachings were so different, that I had to take the last half of the 8th grade over in order to go to the high school. I went to the high school for three months. You can't imagine how different and difficult it was to be in a large public high school after going to a small private school.

After the three months, I begged so hard, that Mama let me quit school and go to work. I was only fifteen, so I had to have a work permit. I first got a temporary job in an office for six weeks for the sum of $10.00 a week. I gave it to Mama and she gave me fifty cents a week to spend. She fixed my lunch and paid my carfare. I felt rich. I had never had that much to spend. Mama worked in a sweet shop. But even with my income, Mama was barely making it. Later, I went to work in a shoe factory where I worked piece work and got up to $21.00 a week.

My older sister Margaret, who was married then, lost her baby. The baby was stillborn. Margaret had uremic poisoning and almost died, so Mama had to go to Lexington, taking my youngest sister Catherine with her. Anthony stayed in Owensboro with Grandma. Louise and I stayed by ourselves because we had to work.

While Mama was gone, the company that Louise worked for gave an excursion down the Ohio River for the employees. I went with Louise, and we took a friend of ours with us. As we were walking on the deck, three boys who were sitting there, called out to us, and we stopped to talk. Later, I sat down by the most handsome one, whom they called "Papa Herman." He wore a derby hat, and to a young person he looked handsome. I noticed that one of the fellows was all bandaged up, having been in an accident at the plant. My heart went out to him, and I got up and asked our friend Maryann to trade places with me, so we changed seats with each other. They called him "Red" because his hair was red. His real name was Harold Fitzgerald. He took me home that day and made another date with me. The day we met was Harold's 20th birthday, May 25, 1925. I had just turned 16 on January 13th.

We three couples continued dating for a few weeks. The others broke up, but Harold and I continued dating. When Mama came home, Harold and I met her at the train, and because we were so much in love we walked her all the way home, telling her about being in love. It was quite a long walk, too.

Mother was quite concerned since I was so young and had not really dated much. So she insisted I date a least one other boy a week. Every time I did date someone else, when I got home, Harold was there waiting at the door.

Within a month, he got a ring and asked me to marry him. I remember my boss asking me (when I showed him the ring) what my fiance's name was. I said, "Red". Then he asked me his last name and I told him I didn't know! I was so much in love that names didn't matter. We planned to wait two years, before we married. Soon we changed it to Christmas, then Thanksgiving.

Finally we got married on the 19th of August 1925, less than three months after we met. Mother found out that we were planning to run away and get married, so she gave her consent.

We were married in the priest's parlor with Mother and Harold's daddy present.

When we got married, Harold had $4.00 left of his paycheck.

Mama gave us the first week's board free. Two days after the wedding, he went back to work. I took the money and got him two blue work shirts and two suits of underwear. He really needed them, but he had a fit when he got home, because we had no money until the next pay day.

The first month after I was married, I cried when I found out I wasn't going to have a baby. Well, I did conceive the next month and had a little girl on June 1st, 1926. We had just been married 10 months. We named her June, as she was born on the first of June. On June 19th, 1927 her little brother was born.

He only lived two months. He was a beautiful baby, but was born with a club foot and internal injuries. He died on August 21st that same year. On August 2nd, 1928, I had another little girl, whom we named Betty. Then on January 4th, 1931, I had another little boy. We named him Harold Lawrence but called him Larry.

September the 16th, 1932, we had another boy, whom we called Bobby. At 23, I had five children, and my life was filled with baby bottles and diapers.

When Bobby was in school, I took a job in a tie factory for two years. Harold worked for what was then U. S. Foil. It was the mother plant of Reynold's Metal. He made $20.00 a week, and with overtime it came to $25.00. I don't remember the exact dates, but I do know he left before the union came in, so he never earned much there. In 1937, Louisville had a big flood, and we had to move out of the house into a school. The plant was filled with water, and so much of the machinery was ruined that they laid Harold off. He was told to go to Richmond, Virginia, and work in their plant there. So, he came to Richmond in 1938.

I stayed and sold all of our furniture. Mama sent us $75.00 to help us move. Harold bought a Model A Ford coupe with a rumble seat and came back for us. We started over again. We rented one-half of a duplex on Royal Avenue in south Richmond for $15.00 a month. After a couple of years, we found a little new house on Wamsley Boulevard, and since it rented for $25.00, we moved in.

All during our married life, as soon as work was over Harold would go to the airport and work until dark. He worked on planes for different people. One day he met a lady who owned a plane.

He did the work that was needed, and she in return, let him use it to take flying lessons. He taught himself to fly with very little instruction.

While we lived on Wamsley, several things began to develop.

Harold quit Reynolds and went into flying. After taking a refresher course, he began to teach people to fly.

CHAPTER 3

God's Drawing to Salvation and Overcoming Temptation

"The Lord hath appeared of old unto me, saying, Yea, I have loved thee with an everlasting love: therefore with loving kindness have I drawn thee." Jeremiah 31:3

After we moved to Richmond in 1938, Harold started going out with other women. My heart was broken, because he had been my life. Even though he was not home much, I had always trusted him. At that time when I needed help so desperately, a knock came on my door. It was a lady that I did not even know. She introduced herself and said that the ladies in that subdivision had decided to start a club so they could get to know one another. Since Bobby, my youngest son, was in the fourth grade at that time and I was lonely, I decided to go with them.

I will never forget that first meeting, there were seventeen of us. While discussing what kind of a club to have, one of the ladies said that if we started with prayer and read one chapter in the Bible each time, the club would stay together. I remember looking around at the others. I thought only Catholics talked about their religion. But even though I was a Catholic, I had been out of the Church for fifteen years, living as though God did not exist. So we started our meetings with prayer and a chapter from the Bible. Then we had dinner and sat around and gossiped.

One day, Ruby, the lady that suggested the prayer and Bible reading, brought one of the plainest people I had ever met, to the meeting. She said that she was going to tell us something about the Bible instead of us reading it. Well, she made that Bible live for us. Her face was no longer plain, because it shone with the Glory of the Lord.

From week to week she came to teach us. In order to get there, she first had to walk one and one half miles to a train station. She then took the train to the center of town, and took a street car for a long ride. Finally taking a trolley that went to a Dupont plant, she would get off and walk two miles to our meeting place. She had her two little children with her. How the Lord used her! Many souls will be in heaven because of her.

She is my friend Gladys "Glad" Billings to whom this book is dedicated.

One day I went to the class and for some reason Glad couldn't make it. Another lady gave us the lesson. Because I was going through a very special trial at that time, when she quoted Psalms 118:8 & 9 it leaped out at me. I had just had my faith in a person badly shaken. But Psalms 118: 8 & 9 said to me, "It is better to trust in the Lord, than to put confidence in men. It is better to trust in the Lord than to put confidence in princes."

From this point on, things got worse, but God, knowing that the time had come for me to be saved, kept Glad on John 3:16.

Her message was, "For God so loved the world that He gave His only begotten son, that whosoever believeth in Him should not perish but have everlasting life," week after week.

One day I knew that I could not go on alone, so I walked down to the creek near my house. Getting on a large rock in the middle of the creek, there Jesus Christ met me. I lifted my heart to Him in faith and He came down and embraced me in His love and gave me His peace. I've never forgotten that day!

At our next club meeting Glad, our Bible teacher, felt led to give an invitation. I thought my heart would jump out of my body. I didn't know what an invitation was. So even though it took everything in me to stay in my seat, I did not respond.

When I had been in the ladies' class about a year, I found out that I was pregnant. Bobby was nine at the time. I was really sick. Rose, one of my neighbors, would take me to her house to take care of me, but I would slip out and go back home.

About the same time, Harold was offered a job at an airport in Maryland. As I was moving away, the ladies made me a scrapbook of memories plus showering me with hankerchiefs, pinning each one on me as I closed my eyes. Harold's employer was to build us a house. I sent the two girls to their grandmother in Kentucky. The two boys were sent to their other grandmother in Florida. I put my furniture in storage and prepared to go to Florida to be with my mother and sister there.

The day came to leave. I took a train to Washington, D. C., and I stayed for a couple of days with Harold at the place where he boarded. I was to leave on the train to Florida on Sunday night. We went to the zoo that afternoon and I missed my train.

And as the Lord would have it, on Monday morning I received my first Bible in the mail from Glad. I took the train that night for Florida.

While at Mama's house, I would cry so much. I did not know what was wrong, because I was not a person that often cried.

When I went to the movies with the children I could laugh with them, so I figured there could not be too much wrong with me. I would open my Bible to read, but if I heard someone coming, I would stick it under the bed. I was ashamed to be caught reading it, because Catholics were not encouraged to read the Bible.

After one month, Harold came after me, because he decided he wanted to go back to Richmond to live. We left and stayed with some friends until we found a house. We soon found a house across town on Waverly Boulevard. For $40.00 a month, it was the nicest home we ever had.

After we moved there, our marriage began to get even worse.

Just before my little one was born, I could not sleep so I got up. Since it was cool, I slipped on Harold's sweater. In the pocket I found something that confirmed my suspicions that he was seeing someone else.

He was teaching flying then, and a girl named Gwen came to take lessons. At first he would come home and tell me how crazy she was. Later, he quit talking about her, because she had finally won him over. He went with several girls, but she was the one he always held on to. He went to see her as long as he was able. During my pregnancy, I felt broken-hearted. I spent a lot of my days in bed not even answering the phone.

The birth of my little one was a nightmare. I no longer felt secure. I was so miserable, and fearful! I felt that Harold had abandoned me, even though we were still living together. The baby was a boy whom we named Mark. He was born on January 15, 1942. The Lord was good. Betty, who was around 16 at the time, stepped in and took care of Mark. The time of agony I went through then was terrible, but necessary in order to have me place my trust in God alone.

Mama came to be with me when Mark was born. She stayed a month and while she was there, she started to read my Bible, so I began to read it, too. After she left, Glad started coming over to my house and listening all day to my troubles, just to get in five minutes of Bible reading and prayer with me. One week I lost 17 pounds. She would try to get me to eat by feeding me with a spoon. Gradually, with Glad's loving patience, I also began to hunger for God's Word. I would read awhile, then throw down my Bible and have a good cry, thus relieving the tensions.

One day I finally came to the end of myself. I had made such a failure of my life. I was standing by my washing machine at that time, trying to wash clothes. I told the Lord if He could do anything at all with my life, He could have it. He took me at my word and began to work with me and still does. At this point He became Lord of my life!

From then on I began to grow in the Lord. But at the same time, many temptations came my way. Some of my husband's friends, who knew that Harold was running around on me, tried to date me. The Lord was good to me in protecting me, as I was too broken-hearted to want to go out with anyone at the time.

I went through all the steps of a jealous woman, going through all his things to see what I could find out, only to hurt more. I had always prided myself on the fact that I was not a jealous person. But after I discovered Harold's affairs with other women, jealousy took control of my life until I turned it over to Jesus Christ. Then He began to lead me out, step by step. "Without me ye can do nothing." John 15:5b

I have never found the Lordship of Jesus Christ to be demanding or hard, and Jesus tells us that His "yoke is easy and His burden is light". Matthew 11:20. As I accepted Him as Lord, He did not burden me down with, "Don't do this and don't do that". Certainly there were things in my life that needed to be changed. But Jesus led me in such a precious way of filling my life so full, I did not need the "don'ts."

I had not been saved much more than a year and had really not surrendered very long, when Harold wanted me to go with him to another couple's house on Saturday night. We proceeded to play cards and drink beer. (Remember I had begun to study my Bible). At midnight, there came a voice in my mind that said, "This is the Lord's day, are you going to finish that beer?" I finished it.

On the way home, I felt disheartened, so I opened the car door and jumped out. I had the thought that if I hurt myself, maybe Harold would show some concern for me. Harold stopped the car and came to help me. When he saw I wasn't hurt, he got disgusted with me, parked the car, and went to bed. I felt so alone. I looked in the glove compartment of the car and got Harold's revolver and walked one-half mile down the road to the woods with the intention of killing myself. Well, I sat there for a long time, and then I went home. I was disgusted, because I didn't even have the courage to kill myself. Now I believe that Satan was trying to destroy me, but instead, God preserved my life.

The next morning, I could not get out of bed and was there three days and nights. God had a chance to deal with me and somehow I knew He did not want me to ever drink again. That night, when Harold came home, I told him I didn't think the Lord wanted me to drink again. He said, "You won't ever quit." I said, "I don't know, but I do know He doesn't want me to drink."

The next day, Harold bought a bottle of Blackberry wine, my favorite, and put it by my bedside table, and put twelve bottles of beer in the refrigerator. Before this we had never kept alcoholic beverages at home. We would go out to drink. Every night he checked the bottle of wine and counted the bottles of beer.

I can truthfully say from that day to this, that I never took another drink. Only once was I ever tempted to drink.

Years later, when I had been working in the garden all day, I came in hot and tired. Needing something to drink I went to the refrigerator and there was a bottle of beer. Was I tempted! I managed to shut the door and get a glass of water. I believe if I had yielded, I would have continued to drink. Praise be to Christ Jesus the Lord! He gave me the strength to resist the temptation.

I heard Glad say one day, "If you are really saved, and continue to live in the same way, you will have such a tug of war going on within yourself." There is no chance of happiness.

Satan will try to pull you one way and the Lord the other, and the one you yield to is your master. While Satan can't take away your salvation, he can make your testimony of no avail, and you will be saved, "so as by fire." "I beseech thee therefore, brethren, by the mercies of God that ye present your bodies a living sacrifice holy, acceptable unto God, which is your reasonable service." Romans 12:1

I had always loved to dance, but as Harold didn't care for it, we seldom did. At this period he began to want to go to dances. One Saturday night we went to a dance. While dancing the thought came to me, "How crazy can you get, a bunch of grown people running around the floor to music." Silly? Yes. But it happened to be the way God used with me, to lead me into deeper things. "And be not conformed to this world but be ye transformed by the renewing of your mind, that ye may prove what is that good and acceptable, and perfect will of God." Romans 12:2

CHAPTER 4

Surrendering My Will For His

"Nevertheless not my will, but thine be done" Luke 22:42a

One day Glad and I were having prayer together. I was pleading with the Lord to save Harold. The Lord began to deal with me, asking, "Would you be willing to give up Harold in order for him to be saved?" I had quite a battle on my knees.

One reason, I wanted my husband saved, was that we could go forth as a happy family, making it easier for me. I struggled quite a bit until I told the Lord I wanted Harold saved, even if I never saw him again. Then the Lord gave me such peace with full assurance that he would be saved. When things got harder, I would always remember, that no matter how impossible things looked, He had given me His promise. I knew that day would come.

Glad was a precious one. She would come over to spend the day with me. If she heard me say something with resentment in it, she would help me to see what was wrong. She also showed me that my resentment was hurting me more than the person I was resenting.

Once I remember going to the attic for something and finding a box with a beautiful nightgown. Harold had broken up with Gwen his girl friend at the time, and when confronted, he said, "Well, I might as well give it to her, because I'm not mad at her anymore!" It hurt deeply, but you know in later years, the Lord showered me with many beautiful gowns.

*****

My little son Mark, who was about two years old at this time, had quite a vocabulary. Everyone said he was too young to talk that well. One day, some men were working on the street and Mark was out there talking to them. They were amazed and they started asking him questions. I looked out the window and could not help but think of Jesus in the temple. His daddy took him riding one day. He was singing little Bible choruses. His daddy said, "Let me teach you a song, "Red Hot Mama." With the wisdom of a child, Mark said, "Daddy, that's a devil's song," and refused to sing it.

Another time, he prayed the most beautiful prayer, and by the temptation from Satan, I had the desire to laugh so much, that I had to leave the room. I was sorry that I had laughed because I never heard him pray like that again. Even though he was small, he was in all my Bible classes with the children. I am sure that the seed of the Word is planted in his heart. When I found out I was pregnant with my next child, I dedicated him to the Lord. In 1945, when Jimmy was born, we started walking to a little mission church just down the road from us. One Sunday afternoon while we were there, an old grey-headed man walked up to the baby carriage and said, "This one is going to be greatly used of the Lord." I couldn't help but think of Simeon at the temple.

*****

As I grew in the Lord, one day the Lord revealed to me that I was judging someone for a sin, that I myself had been guilty of before I was saved. The Lord told me I was to confess my sin to everyone to whom I had gossiped. I remember the sick feeling that came over me. I was to go to a cottage prayer meeting that night, and I felt the Lord wanted me to start there. I walked the floor all afternoon really fighting a battle. I felt no peace in my heart. That night things began to go smoothly, so I thought maybe I was mistaken. But when they read the scripture, "Confess thy sins one to another," I was certain about what the Lord wanted me to do.

Somehow, the Lord gave me the right words to say, so that the ones that did not really know the situation misunderstood, but the ones to whom I had talked, knew only too well. After that, it was easier to go to different ones. But I sure had to call, go see, and write letters to many people.

I've always been told that gossip will spread like wild fire. It is like a pillow emptied of feathers. If we would only realize, how much harm we do with our mouths and how impossible it is to stop all the harm we have done, a lot of pain could be stopped. No wonder the Lord led James to write a whole chapter on the tongue. We need to pray, "Set a watch, O Lord, before my mouth; keep the doors of my lips." Psalm 141:3

Being a new Christian, I had so much to learn (still do) and learned mostly through experiences. The Lord would always, reveal His will through His Word. I determined to put in one hour of Bible study a day, using a book named *The Bible As It Is For Men As They Are*, by Harlin J. Roper. It had 20 questions for each lesson with only scripture references. You had to write down your own answers. Then, I took another hour for prayer and one hour for just reading the Word. I carried on this form of Bible study through the book of Psalms. As a Christian, I was learning that it was so important to hide the Word in my heart.

*****

Once, while praying aloud, I thanked the Lord that I had such peace, and that I was thankful that I was not like my neighbor, who worried so much. Then, I heard someone walk off the porch and I knew she had heard me. Well, this is how the Lord worked it out. For about two weeks everything worried me.

I was upset over everything. I cried to the Lord and He restored my peace. He showed me that it was nothing I had done, but only through His grace did I have such peace. I had begun to assume too much spiritual pride, and He had to take me down a notch or two.

About this time, He started dealing with me about going to church. I went back to the Catholic church, but I wasn't comfortable. I started looking for another church. I decided to try Immanuel Baptist Church, where Glad went. The first Sunday I went to church there, the pastor had a blackboard up on the platform and was describing something about the tabernacle. I knew that was of the Lord, because I had just been studying the tabernacle. He later said that he felt led to do it that day.

He never used the board like that again. That morning he answered the very questions I had in my mind.

Isn't it miraculous, how God works in a Christian's life, when we are seeking His will? I have learned over the years how much the Lord can do when we say, "Not my will, but Thine be done."

Soon after I started going to Immanuel Baptist Church, they had a revival. When they gave the invitation, I knew then what I needed to do. I had already placed my faith in Jesus Christ as Lord and Savior. Now I gladly made a public profession of faith and expressed the desire to follow my Lord in baptism.

What a glorious experience! Truly my joy in Christ was multiplied, for my children—Betty, Larry, and Bobby also made a profession of faith and were baptized. Baptism is a beautiful picture of the death of the old life and the birth of a new life in Jesus Christ.

CHAPTER 5

The Lord Speaks to Me About Being In Debt

"But my God shall supply all your need according to His riches in Glory by Christ Jesus" Philippians 4:19

Harold was everything to me; he came first before anyone.

I guess you would say he was my "god." Before knowing about the adultery, I felt he could do no wrong. His word had always been law in our house. Up until this time, my walk with the Lord had not bothered him. In fact, it made it easier for him to do the things he wanted to do.

I was really in earnest about studying my Bible at this time, and the Lord was about to bring the first test in my life, to see where my real allegiance was.

We, like most people, were in debt. Each payday I would pay our bills, and barely have enough to make it until the next payday. Sometimes we would get a bank loan, pay off all our bills and before long, we would accumulate more. It was a vicious cycle.

I had just completed paying off our loan, and the man at the bank thanked me. He told me to come back, if I ever wanted another loan. I told him that the Lord had shown me not to borrow again. He just looked at me.

You see the Lord had given me the verse, "Owe no man anything but to love one another," Romans 13:8. The Holy Spirit had impressed that verse on my heart and I knew He was talking to me about it.

Well, the time came when Harold was to leave for Florida to go to his new job. It was during World War II and Harold was to teach "dog-fighting" to the Royal Air Force. You can imagine his surprise and anger when he asked me to run to the bank and borrow the money for the trip. I told him I was sorry, but that the Lord told me I was not to borrow any more money. After calling me a poor Christian, etc., he made the statement that I wasn't going to hold him back from that job. So he went to the bank for the loan.

I asked the Lord to control matters. As the Lord would have it, they refused the loan. So when payday came, he paid the rent, got some groceries and took off. He really thought that he would be able to send me some money as soon as he got paid.

However when he got there, they placed him in flight school at half pay and held back the first two weeks pay.

Christian living was beginning to be a real adventure. The Lord had given me Philippians 4:19, "But my God shall supply all your need, according to His riches and glory in Christ Jesus."

June, my oldest daughter, was working as a waitress at the time. She would bring home her tips and give them to me. One day I said that the Lord was supplying all our needs. She said, "You mean, I am." She wasn't a Christian at the time and could not see the Lord at work.

I asked the Lord to open her eyes so she could see His hand in it. Shortly after that, she came down with the flu. While she was sick, we got to the place, that we were down to a pound of beans and a little coffee. I knew the time had come for the Lord to work!

That morning while the children and I were having our devotions before school, our reading was from Exodus where the Israelites were asking the Lord for meat. When we had our prayers, Bobby, my ten year old son, prayed, "Lord, please send us some meat." I had such assurance that the Lord was about to do something. I was going through the house singing, making up my own songs. My neighbor came over to tell me I had a phone call, so, I went over there.

The call was from Rose, one of my neighbors from the old neighborhood. She was one of the ones from the Bible class on Wamsley. Rose was worried about me, wanting to know if I had gotten a check from Harold. I told her that it was not due until next week, and that everything was fine. We talked for awhile.

As I started home, I saw Perdita and Louise coming down the road.

They, too, were from the old neighborhood.

When I told June they were coming, she said, "Oh, mama, what are you going to give them for lunch?" I told her that we had the beans. Then she asked me, "What will we have for supper?" I told her that the Lord would provide. It was such a joy to see Perdita and Louise. They came in and put down their packages.

While they were getting warm, Mark, who had just started walking, walked over to the packages and pulled out a pound of bacon. I told him to put it back, and that he should not get into other peoples' packages.

They told me that they had brought it to me, and were wondering how to tell me, not knowing how I would take it. I said, "Well, I feel like the Lord sent this to me, but how did you know?" They told me they hadn't been able to sleep for a week. All they could think about was me; so they decided to do something about it. They actually cried when helping me to put away the groceries, when they saw how empty my shelves were.

This was during World War II, 1943, when you not only had to have money, but stamps for certain foods. They brought me peaches, sugar, meats and all kinds of vegetables. Their gift truly was a sacrifice for them. They had to use their stamps, which meant that they did without. Also, they gave me an envelope with money in it.

After we put the groceries away, they shared how the Lord watched over them on their journey to my home. They had stopped at Ella's house to pick up some things. Ella's husband happened to be home. He offered to take them to catch the trolley. They waited quite a while, but the trolley never came. He then took them into Richmond, and here they saw that the trolley had broken down. So they had to take a street car all the way across town, and then walk six blocks to my home. The Lord surely looked after them, since it was January with snow on the ground and unusually cold.

When the children got home, together we rejoiced over all the things the Lord had sent us. Bobby was especially thankful for the meat for which he had prayed.

The same day I had a notice that I had a box at the express office in town. I caught the street car and went to the express office. There was a long wooden box of fruit Harold had sent for Christmas, but had arrived late. Praise the Lord that I had that $1.50 since I had to take a taxi home. As I sat in that cab considering all the blessings of that day, I noticed a card about prayer on the windshield. That was all I needed, I told the story of how the Lord had provided all our needs. The cab driver just looked dumbfounded. When I told him I was so glad that he believed in prayer, he replied he had borrowed the cab. Perhaps the Lord knew he needed to hear about the power of prayer.

Glad was out of town when this happened, so, it not only increased my faith, it increased the faith of those whom the Lord had sent to help me. They had never had anything happen like that before; neither had I. Praise His name! He lives! He cares for His own. Yes, I was learning to trust in God's promises. And now I could say, just as Paul did nearly 2000 years ago, "My God shall supply all your need, according to His riches and glory in Christ Jesus." Philippians 4:19

CHAPTER 6

How the Lord Led in the Tithe

"Bring ye all the tithes into the storehouse, that there may be meat in mine house, and prove me now herewith, saith the Lord of host, if I will not open you the windows of heaven, and pour you out a blessing, that there shall not be room enough to receive it." Malachi 3:10

After I had the assurance that I was saved and realized how blind I had been, I began to call up my friends and tell them what had happened to me. Then, I would ask them if they knew the Lord in a real way. One of my close friends said, "I know what you mean. Yes, I am saved." Surprised, I said to her, "You knew if I had died, I would have gone straight to hell, and you didn't warn me?" She said, "I was afraid that you would get mad at me."

I guess that is why we sometimes fail to witness to others.

However, I am sure if we saw someone on fire, we wouldn't just watch them burn, because we did not want to make them mad.

The Bible was so new to me then. I remember I wanted to know everything I could about this Living Word of God. One day I heard someone say something about the tithe. I asked Glad what that meant. She told me it meant giving one tenth of my income to the Lord.

Well, I really prayed about that, since we could hardly make ends meet. Harold gave me most of his paycheck to take care of all our family expenses. One day I took enough money to get a permanent. As I left the house, I picked up a copy of the Christian Readers Digest. While I was sitting under the dryer I came across an article on tithing. As I read the article, the Lord brought home to me that the exact amount that I had paid for the permanent was what my tithe would have been. I told the Lord if He would help me, I would start tithing, and I did.

Several years later, my pastor had a large banner across the sanctuary saying, "Prove me now saith the Lord." That morning the pastor said, "I challenge you. Let each one that does not tithe, try it for one month. If you do tithe, try giving twenty percent, and at the end of the month we will have a testimony of what the Lord has done for us."

I had a real struggle within myself over that challenge.

The children needed clothes so badly, and yet what I had would not even begin to buy the clothes needed. So, I thought, "I'll go ahead. That money couldn't get their clothes anyway." So, I gave the twenty percent. I entrusted the money to God, but I never could have imagined the blessings that God had in store.

One of the first things that happened was that a lady in our church asked me if I would be offended if she offered me some clothes. She said her boy had outgrown them; and my boys were the only ones she knew that could wear them. The lady had wealth, and the clothes were very nice. Already, her gift to me had exceeded the amount of my offering.

Then Harold's business failed. He would sit at home and worry. In the meantime, because the airplanes were at the airport, they were still charging him rent. He was so depressed, that he did not have the heart to do anything. After a six months stay in California, the owner of the field returned. His lawyer asked the owner what he should do about the overdue account. When he saw that it was Harold Fitzerald's, he told the lawyer just to tell Harold to try to get the planes off the field and there was no charge. The owner had been a close friend of Harold's years ago. Later he married a wealthy lady and their lives had gone separate ways. I believe that the Lord sent him home at just that time. A large debt was wiped out. Praise His Name!

CHAPTER 7

Enduring Temptation

"There hath no temptation taken you but such as is common to man: but God is faithful, who will not suffer you to be tempted above that ye are able; but will with the temptation also make a way to escape, that ye may be able to bare it." I Corinthians 10:13

How wonderful the Lord is. I will never forget the time the Lord made this verse my very own, and it has been mine ever since. Harold was in Florida then. For some time, we had been having marital problems. I remember watching my neighbors across the street. They were a close couple. Every evening after supper, they would come out on the porch and just swing and talk. I missed that closeness and affection. Although I had five children then, I was still lonely.

June came home from work one day and said, "Mama, I want to tell you something and I want you to listen. Tomorrow, I want to take you to town and buy you a new outfit and take you to dinner.

Now, that's not all. I have met this real nice sergeant in the service. He is so homesick for his family and I asked him if he would like to meet you. As you know, Daddy is dating others."

Well, I have never had such a wave of temptation as I had then. Everything in me wanted to meet the man. I walked the floor that night and cried out to the Lord. I was tempted on three counts. First, to get a new outfit was out of this world.

I had worn hand-me-downs for so long. Second, to eat out was a genuine luxury. We hardly had food for the table at that time.

But the real temptation was to meet a nice man who might really show me some kind attention. Satan knew my weakness, and he was gaining a foothold. I was deeply tormented. Then the Lord brought I Corinthians 10:13 to mind. I dropped on my knees and cried to the Lord. I quoted that verse and said, "Lord you promised!" Instantly I felt at peace and the burden of the temptation left me.

The next morning, I went with June. She got me a lovely tweed suit, took me to dinner, but the sergeant did not show up.

The Lord gave me the good and removed what would prove wrong.

Praise His Name, for He not only protected me, but He also mercifully took away the loneliness and filled me with His presence.

About this time, Glad started a weekly Bible class in my home. Several of the neighbors came to accept Jesus Christ as their Lord and Savior through that Bible study. I was so thankful for Glad's patient teaching.

At the same time, many trials and temptations came my way.

I truly believe they were used of the Lord to strengthen my faith. There were times when it was tough to discern what was truly God's will and what was my will. I was young in the Lord and had many lessons to learn. But more than anything, I wanted God's will for my life. So when I thought God was speaking to me, I wanted to obey. I believe, that because this was my heart's desire, Jesus was truly the Good Shepherd of my life.

Still, I had a lesson to learn about the deceiving power of Satan. One Sunday, as I was reading the newspaper, I saw a large ad for people to come to work at the airport. I showed the ad to June, my daughter, and she got a job there. Still I kept thinking about that ad, so, I laid it before the Lord. If it was in His will for me to have the job, then they would hire me; if not, then they would not. I took the civil service test and passed it with flying colors, so they hired me.

When I began working, my youngest daughter, Betty, had some problems with her lungs. The doctor said she should stay home from school and lie down a lot. Mark, my youngest son, was two years old then. Since Betty was sick, she had to keep him in the room with her and shut the door. Elizabeth, my neighbor, felt sorry for her and would cook her a good hot meal at noontime. I gave her twenty-five cents which I know did not cover the cost.

Betty needed so many things, but there was no money. To cheer her up, the neighbors got together and gave her a shower of many beautiful things.

I usually did not get home from work, until six o'clock. I remember how tired I was. Working had given me an appreciation for the work Harold did at the airport. After supper, I would have my prayer time. I needed that quiet time with the Lord.

However, as I look back, I am sure I should have spent more time with Betty. Being alone all day, I know she needed companionship. I am sorry that I was not more sensitive to her needs then.

Yes, I have grown as a Christian. I have had some failures as well as victories. I thank Jesus, my Lord, for His forgiving, cleansing love.

After weeks of work, my employer wanted us to go to Pennsylvania for three months training. The only way I could go was to give up our home and sell the furniture. Rose, a friend of mine, agreed to take Betty and Mark to stay with her until I could get settled. I even had to use my tithe to buy the train tickets for my two boys and myself. Here I was, going to a new place with two small children without any money. But I felt that if the Lord sent me, He would provide. The night before we left, the two boys and I went to spend the night with Elizabeth.

Glad heard that I was leaving and had her husband, George, drive her over to see me. I am sure she had little hope that I would stay after selling everything. However, she was convinced that my move was not in the Lord's will. She had seen Satan get hold of other Christians and lead them out of God's will. We talked and had prayer together. Although we were to take the morning train, the Lord used her to show me the error of my ways.

I yielded to the leading of the Holy Spirit. Looking back, I believe that Satan had subtly convinced me that pursuing a career was God's will, when it really was not. Truly we did have financial needs, but God would meet these in His own good way. After all I had done, I took a turn about face.

I went home with Glad that night, leaving the boys with Elizabeth. I stayed one day to rest, then called Elizabeth to meet me in town. We went to the real estate office and re-rented the house. Then, we went to several furniture stores looking for used furniture. Finally, we got to one store, and I picked out the necessities. Praise the Lord, the stove and refrigerator came with the house, and the table, benches and cabinets were built in, so I did not have to buy anything for the kitchen. I noticed the puzzled look on the salesman's face. When I got outside, I remembered he was the man to whom I had sold my furniture! I could not help it, but I had to have a good laugh.

Right after that, Harold came back from Florida, before the

house was finished. I can see him now, going from room to room, shaking his head at what he saw. But since I was seeking to do what the Lord desired, He honored what I was doing. Little by little, the Lord helped me fix up my house and in the end, it looked nicer than before.

What did I learn from this? I learned that obedience to God's will for my life gave a true abiding happiness. In the Christian life, there will be trials and temptations. But James 1:2-4 says, "My brethren count it all joy when ye fall into divers temptations; knowing this, that the trying of your faith worketh patience, but let patience have her perfect work, that ye may be perfect and entire, wanting nothing."

Those were wonderful days, in as much as I saw the Lord answering so many of my prayers. As I was trying to fix up my house, I needed some kitchen curtains. So I asked the Lord for some. A friend gave me two pair of faded green curtains. They were good curtains, but so ugly and faded. When getting the groceries, I planned to get some yellow Rit dye for fifteen cents. At that time money was scarce for me. I had to go six blocks to the grocery store. So, I put the curtains in bleach water while I was gone. I forgot the Rit. But when I took the curtains out of the bleach water, they were the most beautiful canary yellow curtains. They remained that color, as long as I had them at the windows. I told everyone that the Lord dyed them for me.

Another day, I was cleaning my living room. As I was working on my hardwood floors, I said, "Lord it sure would be nice if I had a rug for this room." Fifteen minutes later, Mrs. McClaning came over. Talking to me while I was working, she asked, "Fitzgerald, do you want my dining room rug? I was going to put my new rug over it but the rug stuck out. I was beginning to cut it off, when Leslie said, 'Why don't you give it to Mrs. Fitzgerald?" When I told her that I had just been talking to the Lord about wanting a rug, she could not believe it. Again her faith and mine were deepened.

Enduring temptation had led me to a closer walk with my Lord. I could see the Lord answering so many prayers. "Whatsoever ye ask, we receive of Him, because we keep His commandments, and do those things which are pleasing in His sight." I John 3:22

CHAPTER 8

God Gives Strength and Wisdom and Continues to Answer Prayer

"Before they call, I will answer; while they are yet speaking I will hear." Isaiah 65:24

One day the insurance man came to collect some money for a policy we had. I told him that if the Lord wanted me to keep my insurance, He would send me the money for it. The man thought I was crazy! Many people thought I was crazy, because I took God at His word. I believed that if God said something, He meant it.

He had said that He would supply all my needs, so He was the one to whom I looked.

When the insurance man left, I got on my knees and told Him about the insurance. While praying, a verse came clearly to me, "Before they call, I will answer, while they are yet speaking I will hear." I got off my knees and looked out the window.

Louise and Perdita were coming to the door. They had a letter from a mutual friend who had moved to Florida. In the letter was five dollars which she had asked them to give to me!

I was still trying to refurnish our home. So one day June brought home a second-hand living room suite, and some material to make slip covers. I went to the Lord in prayer, asking Him to provide someone to make them for me. I knew very little about sewing and didn't even have a sewing machine. It seemed that every time I would pray about it, I would hear Him say, "Why don't you make them?" So, one day I started on them. When I would come to a difficult place, I would lay it aside and do something else, praying as I worked. When the Lord showed me what to do, I would go back to it. Since I had to do all the sewing by hand, the sewing wasn't so good. Still they fit perfectly. When Elizabeth, a seamstress, saw them, she told me that she had never been able to make her slip covers fit like that. I had to give the glory to the Lord, because He really showed me the best way.

We had been painting and fixing up the house and those slip covers really looked nice in the living room. At this time I had a Child Evangelism class once a week in my home. I remember the first time I had the class after making those slip covers. Three little five year old boys and Mark, my one year old son, were wiggling around on my new slip covers. I just could not get my mind on the lesson, because I was so afraid they would ruin them.

The Lord had to bring me up short and speak to me, "Which is more important, these slip covers or the souls of those little boys?"

After that it never bothered me, as I knew they were more important.

As I taught those little boys, I learned a great deal. One day Charles came up to me after the class, and wanted to know how your heart could be black as sin, and you put Christ's red blood on it, and it came out white as snow. I had to think on that one for awhile. Then I asked him if he had ever seen his mother take a bunch of dirty white clothes and put them in the wash tub, take a bar of yellow soap, rub it on them, and have them come out white? He said, "Oh yeah, now I see. So that is how it is."

On another occasion, as I was on my way to church, I met Charles and his mother. They were going to the picture show along with several others. He fell behind and started to walk with me. Looking down, he said, "I'm going to the show. Would Jesus like that?" I said, "Do you think the Lord would like the picture you are going to see?" His face lit up and he said, "Yes ma'am, He loves Roy Rogers," and he happily skipped up with his mother. They were precious boys, and I loved them.

About this time I got the house completed and it really looked good. The local church was having cottage prayer meetings, so I offered to have one in my home, even though I didn't go to that church. The people brought chairs from the church, and I cleared one room. I never expected so many people. I am sure some came out of curiosity, but I took them around and showed them the house. It looked lovely.

****

After I was saved, I was burdened about my family. Whenever I would write to any of them, I would always put a scripture verse at the top of the letter and share what the Lord had done for me.

One morning, I woke up with strep throat. I was so sick that I had to stay in bed for several days. I got a letter from Margaret, my oldest sister. She was offended by my witness, and she complained that I was keeping Mama upset. It really hurt, especially since I was sick anyway. The Lord burdened my heart to respond to her letter. At first I felt too sick and weak to write; however, the Lord was persistent, so I finally asked the children to bring me a writing tablet. As I sat up in bed and began to write, I felt as well as anyone.

I started writing in Genesis and stopped in Revelation, pointing her to Christ. I am sure that it was the Holy Spirit writing through me, because I would never have been able to do it. As I lay back down, I was as sick as ever. The Lord surely had helped me. I had the children mail the letter, but I never received a written reply.

Years later, Margaret had what she thought was a minor problem. She went to the doctor, and he said that she needed some surgery. When they operated on her, they found cancer. So the doctor gave her radium treatments. While she was receiving a treatment, he was called to another patient. Due to this distraction, she received excessive radiation. From that day on, she was never well. The doctor said that it was a bad radium burn and was treating her for that. About eighteen months later she was found to have uranium poisoning. Surgery revealed that her cancer had spread throughout her body.

While Margaret was so ill in Georgia, I was in Virginia in the hospital for a miscarriage. Since I had never heard another word from her after I had written her that letter years ago, I didn't know if she was saved or not. So I asked a dear friend of mine, Louise McCraw, whom the Lord had used to start the Braille Circulating Library, to pray for my sister. She told me that she had a friend in Atlanta, and she would write Evelyn and ask her to go see Margaret. Evelyn McClusky was used of the Lord to start the Miracle Book Club, an organization to reach out to teen-agers. The Miracle Book was the Bible. Since Evelyn didn't know what hospital Margaret was in, she went to each hospital until she found her. She talked with the nurses and was told that no one was allowed to see her except the immediate family. Evelyn got Margaret's phone number. She got Mama on the phone and offered to send flowers to Margaret. Mama told her that Margaret didn't like cut flowers, preferring to see them growing in the yard. So Evelyn asked Mama if she could take her to lunch one day, if she hired a nurse to sit with Margaret. Mama said that she just could not leave Margaret. After talking a while, Mama said, "You believe just like my daughter in Richmond." Evelyn told her that she would have her prayer group pray for Margaret.

A couple of weeks later, Evelyn called Mama again. When Mama heard her voice, she told her that a wonderful thing had happened, and thanked her for praying for Margaret. She said that one day Margaret sat up in bed and said, "You all are not telling me what is wrong with me, but it is alright. God has been dealing with me, and I am ready to go anytime." Before this happened, she would get upset with everyone except Mama. After that, she couldn't love them enough. She lived just long enough for people to see the change in her. Her heart was resting in Jesus, and oh, what a difference that made.

I wasn't able to go to the funeral. I did not hear of Margaret's conversion until the following summer. Evelyn McClusky came to Richmond, where we attended a meeting together.

With joy, she told me of her conversations with my Mama. Even though Evelyn was never able to see Margaret, the power of prayer had helped bring her to faith. After learning of her change in behavior and peace in the face of death, I knew she had placed her trust in Jesus Christ.

I was so thankful for Evelyn. She cared enough to do all that she could do to bring my sister to the Lord. I know my prayers, and the prayers of the group, had reached heaven.

What's more, those prayers were answered in a wonderful way.

I cannot tell all the times that the Lord has answered my prayers, but I can tell you that the Lord cares about all of our needs. From slipcovers, to the salvation of loved ones—there is nothing too little, nor too big, for the Lord. There are no limits to God's love and care. He tells us to commit all of our cares to Him.

"Be careful for nothing; but in everything, by prayer and supplication, with Thanksgiving, let your requests be made known unto God. And the peace of God, which passeth all understanding, shall keep your hearts and mind through Christ Jesus." Philippians 4:6-7

CHAPTER 9

The Keeping Hand of the Lord

"Now unto Him that is able to keep you from falling, and to present you faultless before the presence of His glory with exceeding joy." Jude 24

Many people were saying, "Why doesn't she move into a cheaper house if she is so poor?" So, I took it to the Lord and saw an ad in the newspaper for a place that rented for twenty five dollars a month. At the time I was paying forty dollars. Glad cautioned me that I should be sure that it was the Lord's will for me to move. She said that if the Lord wanted me to stay, He would supply the rent.

Because I wanted the Lord's will, I looked for the most impossible sign. It was a beautiful day, and the fruit trees were in full bloom. So, I said, "Lord if you don't want me to move, send so much snow that I will not be able to go", and we went on to church. After church, Bobby came in and said that it was snowing. We went home, and it snowed all day and night! I was glad to know God's will about the house, but little did I think of all the fruit that was killed through that sign. We need to consider all things when we pray. God is able to reveal His will to us in ways that won't cause harm to other people.

Difficult times were at hand. Harold was involved with Gwen. She came first in his life, and he really loved her.

Because of all the hurt, I wanted to separate myself from him.

He told me that it was all in my imagination, so I said, "Alright, I will take your word for it; but I am going to ask the Lord to show me, and if I ever see the two of you together, I will know I am to separate myself from you." One night, the Lord spoke to me telling me to go to a certain place. I had to take two street cars and walk down a dark country road for one-half mile in order to get there. I took a book along to read and to keep my mind off the problem. When I got there, I saw his car parked down the field in front of a little club house at the airport. I walked up to the car. Harold and Gwen were there.

When I spoke to them, they jumped. They didn't know how long I had been there. I said to her, "You've had everything you ever wanted in life, haven't you, Gwen? Well, now you want Harold and you can have him." She started crying.

Then I told Harold that I would not make it hard for him, and I would try to rent out part of the house. With that, I walked away and went back home. I packed everything he owned in boxes and put them on the porch. I intended to call a cab and send it to his work. However, I never could get a cab, so I let them sit there. I even threw away all the pictures I had of him, so there would be nothing to remind me of him. He came back three days later. He never did move out, but for a time I did separate myself from him.

One night he came in and forced me to go into the living room. In the fireplace were all my Bible study books engulfed in flames. As I lay on the couch, I broken-heartedly cried unto the Lord. Then to my amazement, I looked up and saw the Lord suspended in the air above the fireplace. In the vision, the children and I clung together, while the wind whipped around us.

I was holding Mark in my arms and a bat fell in front of one of my children's feet. I will never forget that revelation. I praise His name for His presence in all these experiences. For in the midst of the heartache and despair, I grew to know my Lord better.

In 1945, when Mark was two years old, I found out that I was expecting another child. I made a dreadful mistake while I was carrying the child. I prayed for a little girl. I was so sure that I would have a girl that I wrote the girl's name on the announcements. When he was born, June had to mark out the girl's name and write in the name James. Of course, when James was placed in my arms, he was the most beautiful one. I never regretted that he was a boy, but for a time, we would jokingly tell about this incident. Then one day as we were having family devotions, Jimmy, my little boy, prayed, "Please, don't let Mama care that I am a boy instead of a girl." I learned then that Jimmy thought all the time that I was longing for a girl. You will never know how that hurt me. We need to pay attention to what we say in front of our children.

I remember so well the day Jimmy was born. Harold was having to stay at the airport at nights, because during the war, they had to be guarded. I felt at this time that he should be home with me. I became more worried when I passed my due date by nearly a month. The night I got on my knees and told the Lord I would go without Harold, I started labor at 2:30 A.M. My neighbor from across the street took me to the hospital. The Lord was with me all during the labor. I had such peace between each pain, and my baby came much sooner than they expected.

Again the Lord was precious. The doctor said that he would be a nervous baby, but he had a good disposition. The first morning in the hospital, I was lying there feeling all alone. Feeling unwanted, I opened my devotional book, to this beautiful poem,

> He giveth more grace when the burdens grow greater,
> He sendeth more strength when the labors increase;
> To added affliction He addeth His mercies,
> To multiplied trials His multiplied peace.
> When we have exhausted our store of endurance,
> When our strength has failed ere the day is half done,
> When we reach the end of our hoarded resources
> Our Father's full giving is only begun.
> His love has no limit, His grace has no measure,
> His power no boundary known unto men;
> For out of His infinite riches in Jesus
> He giveth and giveth and giveth again.
>   Annie Johnson Flint

How that poem spoke to my heart, so much so, that I wrote dozens of letters, enclosing a copy of it. The Lord spoke so clearly to me through these verses. Therefore, when Harold did come, I was able to face him with peace in my heart.

****

Some time later, as I was reading about the Crucifixion, I wondered why I didn't feel anything. It just seemed like a story, so I asked God to make it real to me. About a week later, Jimmy became sick. He was just a year old at the time and had just been weaned from his bottle. He was so sick and, I could not get him to eat anything. The doctor, who was Jewish, came every day. He would go away shaking his head. He did not have any hope for him.

About this time, the Lord started to speak to me. He said, "Will you be willing to give up your son, that your husband might be saved?" I would say to Him, "No Lord, why should I? He's a grown man and he knows the way." Then in a gentle voice He would say, "I gave my son for you."

Over and over for three days that went through my mind. I cried the whole time. Finally, I told the Lord He could have my son. I released him to the Lord's care. Finally, I knew peace.

When the doctor came the next day, I met him at the door. I told him whatever happened to my baby would be alright, because I had turned him over to the Lord. He looked at me strangely as he went into the baby's room. In a little while, I heard him say, "Praise the Lord. I've had my first bit of encouragement."

It was at least another month before Jimmy began to pull out of it. As the Lord would have it, Jimmy continued to improve.

He is still living and is in his forties. I had such peace, and the neighbors shook their heads and said, "She doesn't know how sick he is." My Sunday School teacher called my neighbor to see how he was doing. My neighbor told her that it was no wonder he was sick. She blamed me for washing his pajamas and putting them back on him the same day. Since I only had two pair, I had no choice. As he would soil one pair, I would wash them and bake them out on top of a little kerosene heater.

While most of the Sunday School class was critical of me for this, one dear lady felt compassion. She took the streetcar to town and another streetcar to my house to bring two pair of pajamas for Jimmy. Her expression of true Christian love sure lightened the load for me. I'll never forget the peace of the Lord as I would rock him in my arms and sing all the precious songs the Lord would give me. Surely it was a peace that passest all understanding. Through it all, I came to have a feeling for what it cost our Heavenly Father to give His only Son for us.

****

June, my oldest daughter, married a serviceman. When Harry, her husband, was sent overseas, she stayed with us. She had a little boy about the time Jimmy was two. When Harry got back from overseas, they lived with us for awhile. Then when we moved, they got a little house near us. Later, they lived in Germany on two different occasions, having a little one each time. They had three little boys in all.

When World War II was over, rents began to jump up, and houses sold for a lot more. Before our landlady could raise our rent, the government instituted rent controls. So the lady sold the house, but she had to give us six month's notice. It was very hard to find a house for sale or rent, but Harold kept on looking. I do give him credit for being determined to get on a bus line so I could go to church.

I began to feel poorly. I went to the doctor and he said it was my nerves. I told him that it couldn't be, because I trusted in the Lord. He said, "I know you do, but you have an inner nervous system that you have no control over." I came home and cried because I felt like I had failed the Lord.

Finally, Harold found an old house on Willis Road in Chesterfield County. The roof was beaten in, no inner walls, just a shell. He borrowed money for a down payment, and we bought it. He would take the older boys to the house, show them what he wanted done, and he would check on them at noon. Then he would come by after leaving his job, and work until dark. At that time, Larry was sixteen and Bobby was fourteen. We moved into the house on the fifteenth of February. We closed off the kitchen and pantry so we could heat them. We put tarpaulins up in place of the doors. We had no electricity. We used a well and an outhouse.

The day we moved, the weather was beautiful. But three days later, we had one of the worst snow storms of the season. We had a difficult time, but we managed somehow. The house was old and crooked. Even though we managed to make it livable, we could never fix it like a real home. The place was covered with broken whisky bottles and honeysuckle was everywhere. We were two hundred feet off of the road and our driveway was nothing but mud. We had to push the car every morning to get it started so Harold could go to work.

Those were hard days, but they proved to be a boot camp for a place to which we moved later. As we cleared the land, the soil was good. I learned not only to garden but to can. Because I had grown up in the city, I know I did everything the hard way, but I did learn. Sometimes it would be eight o'clock at night before I would get the breakfast, lunch, and dinner dishes washed. I would fall in bed at night and pray for strength to get up in the morning. With no time to read my Bible, the Lord brought two portions of verses to my mind:

"...His way is perfect", "...there is no God like thee, in heaven above, or earth beneath," Psalm 18:30a & I Kings 8:23a

One night, by the moonlight I was hoeing my beans. I remember calling out to the Lord, "It just isn't fair." The Lord gently spoke, "Can't you go the second mile?"

As we were settling in the house, I wanted to put the Lord first. So I started a children's Good News Club. My children told other children, and four or five would come. I would stop what I was doing, have the class, and then go back to work. I remember one day I was putting up a stove pipe. With soot all over my face, in came the children. I pulled out a bench, had the class, and then went back to work.

That afternoon as I was walking to the mail box, discouraged and tired, I thought, "What is the use of it all?" The Lord spoke to me, "One day you will tell your story before a large group of children." It came with such a deep inner conviction that this would happen. As time went on, I did have four children's classes and ladies' class. But the promise that I would teach a large group of children was yet to come.

A few years later I joined Kingsland Baptist Church. One day my friend, Betty, was looking for a missionary project. She knew of a home for black children. She approached the people in charge to see if we could put on a program there. The people gave their permission, so she got a group together. Brenda Cole played the piano. Others served the refreshments and sang. I was to give the message on flannelgraph. I chose the story of Adam and Eve.

When we got there, the children just ignored us. Brenda sat down at the piano and began to play. We gathered around her and sang. They watched us for a time. Then one by one they began to come over to the piano, and the ice was broken. There were about sixty children from about five to sixteen years of age. We sang a while, and then it was time for me to tell my story. The Lord was there, even though I was undoubtedly scared. They were so quiet that you could hear a pin drop. After the story, we had refreshments. The children were so nice.

On the way home, Betty told us that she had received word that the week before the children were so disruptive that the leaders could not put on the program. Furthermore, they were planning to do that to us. She had decided not to tell us and asked the Lord to take care of us. Days later, I remembered how the Lord had revealed to me years ago, that I would teach in front of a large group. Many times we can see the handiwork of the Lord clearer as we look back over our lives. We can see how He uses the hard times and the good times to shape our lives.

THE WEAVER

My life is but a weaving
Between my Lord and me
I cannot choose the colors
He worketh steadily.
Oft'times He weaveth sorrow,
And I in foolish pride
Forget He sees the upper
And I the underside.
Not 'til the loom is silent
And the shuttles cease to fly
Shall God unroll the canvas
And explain the reason why.
The dark threads are as needful
In the weaver's skillful hand
As the threads of gold and silver
In the pattern He has planned.
     Grant Colfax Tullar

CHAPTER 10

God's Grace in Our Lives

"Looking diligently lest any man fail of the grace of God; lest any root of bitterness springing up trouble you, and thereby many be defiled." Hebrews 12:15

Two of my greatest sorrows in life were Harold's unfaithfulness and his unbelief. It was only by God's grace that I was able to deal with the strain.

In the early years, I was very bitter. There were times I saw a glimmer of hope. Once when Gwen had moved away and was gone quite a while, the Lord really dealt with Harold. The second was when the Lord used Jimmy to speak to his heart.

I had taken Jimmy and Mark to the Mosque Auditorium in Richmond to hear Jackie Burris, an evangelist. After the service, he gave the invitation for those who wanted to be saved to come forward. We were seated in the back. When I opened my eyes, Mark, who was six years old, had gone down to be saved. Even Jimmy, who was four, looked up at me and said, "I want to be saved," as clearly as he could.

The next morning, Harold and I were talking as we sat at the kitchen table, Jimmy was playing with his tinkertoys. All at once, he looked up and said, "Daddy, you know what this is? It's a cross, and Jesus died on that cross, and Daddy, if you don't believe in Jesus, you will die and go to hell."

On another occasion, when his Daddy was walking around the yard, he walked up to him and said, "Daddy, we love Him because He first loved us." That had been his memory verse for the week.

Harold would take Jimmy on the tractor and drive him around.

Jimmy would tell us that his Daddy had said that he would go to church with us some day. He went to the Mosque Auditorium once.

He also listened to a man on the radio speaking on John 14.

Hope for his salvation awakened in me. Then Gwen came back with her first child and it was all over. He lost all desire for spiritual things.

We had been living in the old house in Chesterfield County about two-and-a-half years when I found out I was pregnant again. Harold knew that it would be hard to care for a baby since we had no lights, so he had the house wired. I was so sick each morning that Harold would clean the house before going to work. He also got a hammock for me.

While having the morning sickness, I also took the flu. One morning as I was going out to lie in the hammock, I happened to walk by our car, and I saw a baby seat in it. I assumed he had bought it for the baby, and I was so excited. I went in to tell him how thrilled I was and to thank him. He said, "Leave it alone, it isn't yours. Quit looking into my things." I remember how my heart sank. At that time I never got to ride in the car.

I even had to take a Trailways Bus to go to the doctor. You can imagine my feelings, lying there in that hammock, sick, knowing that he was taking her out with her baby. As I lay there in despair, it seemed like God sent his angels down to minister to me. I know that God does minister to His own.

****

About this time in our lives, Harold started bringing his male friends to our house for lunch. He was so proud of our fresh vegetables and wanted his friends to share with us. Harold had told them that I was "religious". As they came to know me as an individual person, they grew to like and respect me.

One day when I was near my due date, Harold came home with Don, one of his friends. While Don was there, I started into labor. Don called Peg, his wife, and told her he wouldn't be home. I was so thankful that he stayed because Harold had been drinking. As my labor increased, we decided that I should go into the hospital. Don drove. When we got there, Harold said, "You all go in. I will stay out here and wait." So Don and I went in. The doctor was not there. While we were waiting, my pain lessened. I began to feel foolish about the whole thing.

So I said, "Let's leave." We went out and found Harold asleep in the car. It was all shut up and full of smoke. He had set the car on fire and would have died if we had not come out at that time.

Don put it out as best he could. We got Harold awake and at 2 A.M. drove into a station. We all got out of the car. Don got the water can and poured water on the seat, then Don drove us home.

About three days later, while we were having breakfast, I knew it was time to go. After breakfast, Harold drove me to the hospital. They said it would be quite a while before the baby would be born, so Harold went home. My little boy Tommy was born sometime during the night. This was the second baby that was born without his father being there. He stayed with me all the time with the first six children.

The day Harold brought me home, Don, Peg, and their little girl came to spend the day. Peg cooked the meal. After dinner Harold wanted them to go to the movies with him. Since that would have left me alone with Mark, Jimmy, and the baby, Peg told him, "No, your wife needs you at home." So Harold took them home and came back to stay with me.

One day Don was there when I almost dropped the baby. He ran over in such a way that I thought to myself, "Why, he loves me!" Harold had seen the look that Don had given me. Later when Harold took him out to the car, Harold came back, and looked at me. I think he wondered if I had noticed Don's actions.

After so many years of being pushed aside with no affection shown, you can imagine how this struck me. Here was someone who really loved me. I was overwhelmed. When I knew he was coming by, all I could think of was him. When I was out, I watched for his car. Even though the attraction was great, my Lord protected me from myself. Don respected me, so he never made any advances toward me.

Still, I know Don's feelings were strong. After he would visit us, he would go somewhere and just park and think for several hours. Then when he got home, his wife would accuse him of taking me out. Their little girl was upset by her mother's accusations. She had been with her daddy and knew that he had not been alone with me. Sometimes the little girl would even ask me to talk to her mother and explain things.

In all the emotional turmoil, the Lord convicted my heart that we needed to put an end to the infatuation. So one day when Don and his daughter were leaving, I walked out to the car and told him to go on home to his wife and make their marriage work.

He said, "Well, I'm batting at it." Strangely enough, after that, the temptation left me. I know the Lord's protection was there all the time, since no move was made by either of us toward the other. For I am sure, had one of us made the move, we would have ended up in each other's arms!

****

Through all of this time, Harold continued his affair with Gwen. In the early years I was very bitter. I remember the time when Gwen's first baby was small, and Harold had gone over to her house. I prayed for God to take vengeance on her for what she was doing to my family. A week later when Harold and I were out together, he stopped by her house. I went in with him and found her sick in bed. When she saw me, she said it was just like an angel had come. She said she knew that I would take care of her baby. Gwen had been bitten by a black widow spider. You can imagine how I felt, because I realized that this had happened because of my prayer. I asked the Lord to forgive me and told Him I would never pray that prayer again. I was wrong to pray for vengeance on someone, and the Lord showed me the error of my inner feelings.

A few years later Gwen left again. This time she went to Florida to live. Once again Harold began to open up to spiritual things. Billy Graham was having a crusade in Richmond. I went to counseling school and planned to attend every night. Harold was responding to it, and I had every reason to believe that this time he would really open his heart to the Lord. However, when we pray for the conversion of someone, Satan is bound to bring something to pass to cause things to turn aside.

Then Satan attacked. Gwen's husband, who had stayed at his mother's home in Richmond, came out and told Harold that Gwen wanted to come back to Richmond. He asked if they could stay at our house until he found a place. Of course Harold said they could.

When she arrived in Richmond with her two children, her husband brought them to our house, settled them in, and then he went back to his mother's home. God's grace is wonderful, for I know that I could not have gone through that if He had not been with me. I even kept the children one night and sent her to the crusade. They stayed at our house for six weeks. Because of prayer, the Lord enabled me to live for Him, and I know she saw that. I had always prayed that I would never let bitterness rule me and that maybe one day we could be friends, and I did see that day. I saw the day, I had a great compassion for her and still do.

CHAPTER 11

Following on to Walk With the Lord

"And thine ears shall hear a word behind thee, saying, this is the way, walk ye in it, when ye turn to the right hand, and when ye turn to the left." Isaiah 30:21

We lived in an old house on Willis Road for seventeen years.

Not all the times were hard. Some years our garden flourished, and I canned the bounty. One year we killed three hogs. Once we had twelve hams in the refrigerator, another time we had a bull butchered. It was some of the best beef I ever tasted. We had chickens, too.

One day as I was going to Glad's house, the Lord spoke to me about taking her a ham. I went back and picked out a small one since there was only three in her family at the time. The Lord spoke to me again saying, "Take it back and get a large one," so I obeyed Him.

When I arrived at her home, I placed the bagged ham on her kitchen table. We visited with each other and then said our goodbyes. She did not open the ham until I had gone out to the car, but before I drove away she came out to tell me how that ham was an answer to prayer.

God had been dealing with her about starting a Christian school. Finally, she told the Lord she did not even know how to start. So God had led her to invite fifteen interested couples for supper to discuss the possibility of a school. She had wanted a ham so much, but as finances were tight, she knew that George could not get one. Knowing the desires of her heart, the Lord moved me to take the ham. The supper was the very next evening. As they fellowshipped and talked around that ham supper, the initial ideas for a Christian School developed. The outcome was the establishment of the Richmond Christian School.

I was so thankful that I could offer something to help Glad, since she had helped me in so many ways.

On another occasion, as I was going to a home Bible study, I felt led to put some things in a bag and take them to Lillie, a friend of mine. I had started to put some cheese in several times, but I did not. As she began to unpack the bag of food, she said, "The Lord gave me everything I asked for except the cheese." You can imagine how I felt!

Our Bible study classes were very special. Not only did we grow closer to Jesus Christ, but we also formed lifelong friendships with one another. In one of my classes were Lottie and Lillie. They both wanted their lives to count for the Lord.

After being saved, they were open to the Word and grew mightily.

We were so close that people referred to us as "The Three Musketeers". Later, Kathleen joined us. The four of us were like sisters. There were so many good times in those classes — such rich fellowship. And even though I was the teacher, we were all growing together in the Lord.

I remember when the Lord began to burden me for Lottie. We had bought our home from her husband. She wanted her little boy to learn about the Lord, so she let me have a Good News Club in her home. She was so proud when he learned the Twenty-Third Psalm. I really wanted her to go to an adult Bible study I was teaching at Lillie's house. So I started stopping by to ask Lottie if she wanted to go with me. She told me later that she would dress early so she could leave before I got there. However before she could leave, I would show up and say, "Oh I am so glad you are going with me this morning!" Not wanting to hurt my feelings, she went with me. Today Lottie is still a precious one in the Lord.

At first Lottie's husband was pleased when she turned to the Lord. He had attended church, but she had not been going. He came down and thanked me for getting her to go to church.

However, as she grew, the Lord began to speak to her about certain things in their lives that were not right. When she began to change, it began to convict him of the wrong in his life, and then, he turned against me.

If I went to their house he would grab his hat, and out the door he would go, slamming it behind him. He was as much against me as he had been for me. Several years later when he was in the hospital with cancer, I mustered all my nerve and went with Lottie and Kathleen to see him. On that visit, he politely ignored me. After he came home, he was an invalid. It was during his confinement that I had the opportunity to minister to him a little.

He had ridiculed the small Baptist church near him. Still the deacons took tapes to him regularly. With the aid of those tapes, he had a real experience with the Lord. He had put Lottie through much persecution, but because she stuck by him, the Lord rewarded her, for she knows he is with the Lord today. No case is too hard for the Lord, for He is longsuffering and kind. We need to follow His example, being faithful in our love, witness, and prayer.

****

One time while my mother was visiting, she would listen to Jesse Hendley speaking over the radio each day. He was having tent meetings in Richmond. Quietly, she listened to him. When he said something that was opposed to what she believed, she would ask me about it. Always the Lord would lead me to a verse of scripture that would give her the answer.

One Saturday morning, I took a group of children to the tent meeting while Mother kept the baby. One of the little boys with me used to say, "I'll hide and He won't find me," when I would talk to him about Jesus. Finally, one day he told me he wanted Jesus to come into his heart. Well, that day at the tent, when the invitation was given, he said, "Come on, I want to go down front. I did not come here for all this foolishness. I came to be saved!" He was five years old.

When we got home, Mama was greatly disturbed. She said, "I have to go to Margaret's house tomorrow. Lloyd has just cut his throat and I do not think he is saved." I too was disturbed by what Lloyd had done. But when I heard her express concern over his salvation, the joy bells broke loose in me. For I had never heard her use that expression before. She was always a precious person. She had always believed in God and prayer, but I felt that now her relationship with Jesus had become real. Lloyd lived and years afterwards was saved, too. Margaret, as you know, met the Lord on her death bed.

****

Many times when I would want to go ahead of the Lord, He would turn me to the verse, "Wait on the Lord: be of good courage, and He shall strengthen thine heart: wait, I say, on the Lord." Psalm 27:14

It is true the Lord brought me through some crises in a miraculous way but, as you know, "day by day" trials are often the hardest to face. Sometimes I would dwell on the unfairness of things. When I would be sinking low, I would start to read in my Bible, and just the verse that I needed would be there. "The Lord shall fight for you, and you shall hold your peace." Exodus "14:14 "Dread not, neither be afraid of them. The Lord your God which goeth before you, he shall fight for you," Deuteronomy 1:29b-30a

One time Harold was sure that I did not have to pay all the bills I said I owed. To prove his point, he took me around to each place and gave me the money to pay while he waited outside.

After each payment I would bring him the receipt. He saw that I was right, but you can imagine what that did to my pride. When I got home, I felt so low. I picked up my Bible and it opened to the Thirty-seventh Psalm. The first six verses just leaped out at me. Oh, how it spoke to my heart! Harold also accused me of giving all my money to the church. He knew I did tithe. Trying to prevent me from giving to the church, he gave me less and less money. One day the amount he gave me was about half of what I needed. I got on my knees and asked the Lord what to do. He led me to pay all my bills and mail the receipts to Harold at the airport. When Harold added them up, he saw that I did not have any money for groceries; so he gave me more.

So often it seemed like things were going Harold's and Gwen's way. I felt so helpless. But the Lord would assure me that even though I could not do anything about it, He was working it out. And He did. In loving kindness He drew me to Himself and slowly changed me step by step. What's more He was working in their hearts, too. Even though I had to deal with injustice in my life, I learned to trust in God's promises. "Commit thy way unto the Lord; trust also in Him; and He shall bring it to pass. And He shall bring forth thy righteousness as the light, and thy judgement as the noonday." Psalm 37:5-6

****

In the 1960's there was such turmoil between the whites and the blacks. The blacks were demonstrating and going to the white churches. I was examining my heart one day, and I remember asking the Lord if I had any prejudice in my heart toward the black people. I said, "Lord, even if it means washing a black person's feet, I would rather do that than let anything come between you and me."

Shortly after that a black woman stopped by the door. I asked her in, and we talked. Her name was Alice. She started coming regularly. All she had to do was flatter the children, and they would give her anything she wanted.

One morning around six o'clock, a taxi pulled up and in came Alice. She managed to pay the taxi driver and almost passed out.

Hurriedly, I woke up the boys. They took down their bed and put it up in the living room while I called the doctor. I nursed her back to health. She stayed in our home about two weeks. One day when I was bathing her feet, I remembered my prayer. When we pray a prayer, the Lord brings circumstances that answer it.

On another occasion, I was praying for a neighbor who was sick. The Lord spoke to me and said, "Quit praying and go help her." Sometimes the Lord may answer a prayer by giving us a task to do. The Lord may lead us to put feet to our prayers.

In the same way, I was led to help Mrs. Bates, one of my neighbors. She lived alone and could no longer care for herself. So I started going over at meal times to fix her meals. While she ate, I would read my Bible. One day she asked me to read aloud to her. Eventually she had to be fed. So I would feed her, and then read the Bible to her. Through this care, she was touched by Christ's love and came to a saving knowledge of our Lord.

At that time I began to feel ill. I did not know if I was going through the change of life or was pregnant. I had already had eight children.

One Wednesday night I went over to fix Mrs. Bates' supper.

I worked hurriedly, so I could go to prayer meeting, but Mrs. Bates seemed to want me to stay. I knew that both of her sons and their wives lived right in back of her home. I was sure they would be over to check on her, so I left. As soon as I returned from prayer meeting I went over there. But they had already taken her to the hospital.

I planned to go see her the first thing in the morning, but she died before I could get there. The nurse said that she had been in Mrs. Bates room around five o'clock and she had spoken to her. Returning in ten minutes, she found her dead. The nurse said she had a smile on her face.

Floyd and Clarence, her two sons, made plans to take her seventy miles away for the funeral. It was to be on a Sunday.

However, because Floyd knew that I wanted to be in church, he changed the time to Monday so I could go. It was on March 1st.

The weather was beautiful at first, but later the wind blew hard and cold. I was feeling poorly; but since he had changed the day just for me, I felt I should go. Wilma, her Uncle Charlie, the preacher, and I rode with Floyd in his new Cadillac.

As we rode along, I began to feel worse and worse. Along the way, we stopped at a store and I immediately found a chair and sat down. I felt tired and weak. When we arrived at his cousin's house, I still felt weak and sat the whole time. Then it was time to go to the funeral. When we got to the church, I told them to go on in, and I would come later. After everybody went in, I managed to get into the church and sat on the back seat. I remember looking in the direction of the casket and thinking, "You took a lot out of me in your lifetime and now in your death you are taking more." Taking care of five children at home, and helping her, had left me feeling worn and weary. But I felt that perhaps there was something more seriously wrong with me. I waited until everyone had left the church to go to the cemetery. Then I managed to get back to the car.

I realized then what was wrong with me. I was having heavy bleeding and cramping. So when Floyd got back to the car, I told him to take me somewhere. Since there was no hospital near by, he took me to his cousin's house. As we drove up, Wilma directed me to the outhouse. So as they went into the house, I went to the outhouse. There I had a miscarriage and lost my baby.

Truly, I could not have made it without my Lord. It was a terribly lonely experience. About this time, Wilma came out to see about me. She managed to get me into the house, where I sat next to the kitchen stove. They gave me some clean clothes, and I sat there while they were preparing food for the crowd.

Although I was only about six feet away, I asked them not to invite me to come to the table.

While they were cooking, I began feeling ill again. So they took me to the pantry and put down papers. I guess I passed the afterbirth there. After that they fixed me a place to lie down.

I had never been through anything like that outside the comforts of a hospital. I was reminded of a book I had read the previous winter while sitting by a warm fire. It told how women of another culture would stop on the path, have their baby, then pick them up, and go on. I remembered thinking, "Well, that is one thing I haven't gone through." But now I felt a oneness with those women. It brought to mind the suffering that many people have to undergo all around the world with very little care and comfort. I know Jesus has a special compassion for those who suffer and are oppressed. For He fulfilled this scripture: "The spirit of the Lord is upon me, because He hath anointed me to preach the gospel to the poor; He hath sent me to heal the broken-hearted, to preach deliverence to the captives, and recovering of sight to the blind, to set at liberty them that are bruised, to preach the acceptable year of the Lord." Luke 4:18 19. Jesus is truly an ever-present comfort in times of suffering.

Floyd had to take the preacher back early, so I waited and came back with Clarence. On the way home, I laid down on the back seat. They stopped by a doctor's office, and he gave me a shot to stop the bleeding. When we got back to Richmond, they went to pick up their children. Their friend invited us all in, but I just stayed in the car. They continued to visit for quite a while. However, in all fairness, they did not realize how sick I really was.

When we got to my house, Clarence's wife offered to come in with me, but I told her that I would be alright. The house was cold, since no one was home. But I managed to pull the couch over by the oil stove. I lit the fire and opened the couch.

Down inside the couch, was my Bible. Harold had hidden it from me the previous month.

I was very sick for several days, and Gwen called and begged me to go to the doctor, so Larry took me. I was put in the hospital for a "D and C". I had four heavenly days of rest.

I remember waking up to be so thankful that I did not have to do anything. I know the Lord let me go through that to show me nothing is impossible with God. Truly, we *can* endure all things through Christ who strengtheneth us.

The doctor told me that I should have an operation, so he sent me to a specialist. When the specialist examined me, he told me that if I did not have the operation, I would have advanced cancer in two years. I was already feeling poorly, and that did not help. The doctor wanted to admit me then, but I told him I would have to go home and make arrangements first.

Before I went home, I stopped to see a friend that was in the hospital. While talking with him, I thought, "Why do I want to go into the hospital and be sick like that." So I let things ride for awhile.

Everytime I would pick up my Bible, it would open to a place where the Lord had healed someone. I went to another doctor for a second opinion. He said, there were problems there which would have to be treated, perhaps in at least fifteen years.

I asked the Lord if He wanted to heal me by the doctor's skills or by His hand alone. I kept reading my Bible and one day I read, "I will not give my glory to another." Isaiah 42:8b

So I left it in the Lord's hand and got involved in my classes. In time I forgot all about it. Did the Lord heal me?

Or did He save me from having an unneeded operation? One thing is sure, it is now thirty-five years later and I still have not had any surgery.

Later when I prayed about my ears being healed, He gave me this verse, "My grace is sufficient for thee. For my strength is made perfect in weakness." II Corinthians 12:9a But He has overruled about my hearing. In a way, I guess I have been protected from hearing a lot I should not hear. One thing I know, the Lord never makes a mistake. We can praise His name for that.

CHAPTER 12

Can God?

"For we walk by faith and not by sight:" II Corinthians 5:7

My daughter, Betty, accepted Jesus Christ as Lord and Savior when she was thirteen. When Betty was seventeen years old, she was steadily growing in the Lord, and we were attending Immanuel Baptist Church where they really challenged you to look to the Lord in faith. They had announced a Bible conference that would be held at Keswick, New Jersey. Betty started praying that the Lord would make it possible for her to make the trip. Little by little the money came in which made it possible for her to go. Betty had also been praying for some clothes for the trip. That prayer was answered through a neighbor who had lost a sister. She came over with all her sister's clothes for Betty, who was overjoyed.

They fit her perfectly.

Before Betty left, Mary Louise and Richard, my sister's children, came to spend the summer. They lived in Louisville, Kentucky. The children loved to play in the park and go blackberry picking. Mary Louise was about the same size as Betty. So Betty shared some of her new clothes with her.

Even before Betty left for the conference, Mary Louise had been sick. But after Betty left, she became very ill and began to break out. I called the doctor but he did not get there until two o'clock the next morning. When he examined her, he saw that she had tick fever. It was a new disease at the time, almost always fatal. So we put her in the hospital. She had been infected by a tick which had gotten in her head while picking blackberries. I had everyone praying for Mary Louise; for I knew the same summer there had been two other adult cases of the tick fever, and those people had died.

About this time, Richard started to cry. He said his face hurt, so I took him to the doctor. He had an abscess and I had to put him in the hospital, also.

Mary Louise got so homesick that the doctor told me to send for her mother. So, I called and told her what was happening.

She had her husband in one hospital in Louisville and her married daughter in another one, but she caught the train to Richmond, bringing with her, Raymond, her three year old boy. When she arrived, the children started getting better. Not long after she arrived, Louise's little one became ill with the whooping cough.

Then not only my little one, but the whole neighborhood came down with it. It was a hectic, stressful time.

So much was going on, that when Betty came back all excited about the conference, there was no one to listen. It had been a wonderful experience for her. While there, she had gone forward to commit her life to missions. Many times I have blamed myself that I did not take the time to listen to her.

One day she decided that she wanted to learn to play the piano. We had no piano, nor money for lessons, but she and I began to pray about it. Some time later, there was a knock on the door and a lady asked me if I would be willing to rent her a room for a studio. I rented her the room, and she gave Betty piano lessons. She even gave Betty the key to the room so she could practice whenever she wanted! It truly was a wonderful thing to see the Lord at work in such tangible ways.

These special demonstrations of the Lord's provision built up Betty's faith. So when she graduated from high school, she wanted to go to a Christian college. Again, we went to the Lord in prayer. She sent in applications to several Christian colleges. Finally, she decided to go to William Jennings Bryan College in Dayton, Tennessee. At the time she entered, it was not accredited, but before she left, the school received accreditation.

She began her college studies in faith. She knew that we did not have the money to send her, but the Lord honored her decision and helped us to make a way. First the same neighbor who had brought the clothes for her, came over one day and said, "Well, I sold my house and I brought my tithe to you to help on your college tuition. It was fifty dollars! That was a lot of money in 1944. That was the largest amount she got at one time.

It was not easy, but between what she earned working and gifts from others, she completed all but the last quarter at the college. Then she became ill and had to quit. In later years she did finish.

She met the man she was to marry at Bryan College. The saying about Bryan College at that time was, "Bryan is like a shoe factory. You go in single and come out double."

I remember the letter I received from Betty to tell me that she and Norbert were coming at Christmas and that they planned to get married. She was planning to be married in the church. All I could think of was the reception. I did not know what I was going to do. Harold's business had failed. He was unemployed, and we had very little in savings. I cried to the Lord and said, "Lord, even you can't provide refreshments in a wilderness."

The Lord did not rebuke me for saying that, but He worked it this way. The drive-in-theater across the road from my house was closing down for the season. Bobby was working at the refreshment stand, so when they closed, they loaded him down with refreshments. Since this was in November, I was not able to use them for the reception. But all the children in the neighborhood had parties for weeks and my Lord showed me that He could provide refreshments in a wilderness.

I can remember my husband saying that he was not going to walk down the church aisle for anyone! His friends teased him constantly. Then one day he came home with a new pair of shoes.

Jimmy was five at the time. He said, "Daddy is 'dem' you 'wedden' shoes?" As the time got closer, he told me. "Well, you might as well go with me to get a suit." I went with him and he picked out a tan suit. I wondered if the color would be appropriate for the wedding, but God was there all the while.

Even though they had not consulted one another, the bridegroom and the best man had tan suits, too. Another miracle of our God!

While planning the wedding, Betty and Norbert would get on their knees and pray for the Lord's guidance. First, Jane, her friend, asked her if she would like to use her wedding dress instead of buying one. Then the church gave her a personal shower with all the underclothes she needed. They were praying daily for a check they were expecting to come. So they ordered flowers on the strength of that.

They had planned for Ruth Joy, a classmate from Bryan College, to sing at their wedding. One day Norbert said to Betty, "We have asked Ruth Joy to give up her Christmas to sing at our wedding, and no one has a gift for her." So they took their last $4 and got her a gift. That night at the supper table, Bobby, who had been working at the post office after school, said, "I haven't given you all anything for your wedding, so I will give you five dollars." Norbert jumped up and said, "Whoopee! Now we can get our marriage license!" That was Thursday night. They were to be married on Saturday, Christmas Eve. Friday, Harold came home early so he could take them over to get their marriage license. They got there just before the door was closed. They were so thankful that they made it in time because they were not open on Christmas Eve.

One of the ladies at the church called and wanted to know when the wedding would be over so they could decorate the church for Christmas. Betty told them to go ahead and decorate and she would use it for a background.

Harold and Norbert went to pick up the flowers. Although the check had not come, Harold wanted things to be nice, so he was going to write a check for them. However, when Harold wrote the check, they told him that they did not know him and would not accept the check. They explained to them the urgency of the situation. So the florist called a reference for Harold and then gave approval.

In the meanwhile, at the church everything was ready, and everyone was waiting. The pastor stuck his head in the door and teasingly said, "Don't worry, Betty, I will grab the first man that comes along, and we will go ahead with the wedding."

Finally Harold and Norbert got there with the flowers and the wedding began. It was a beautiful wedding. After it was over, one man said, "I do not see why people want to put on such expensive weddings when they cannot afford it." I had to laugh at that! Since Harold was out of work at the time, most things had come by the Lord's provision.

I had four hens which we killed and cooked. I believe Harold gave me a bushel of apples and a box of tomatoes.

Harold's sister, Opal, and her husband, Buck, came and brought Gracie, their daughter-in-law with them. They had a large bag of groceries. We did very well until most of the company left.

Betty, Norbert, and Ruth Joy stayed until the holidays were over. Betty took Ruth Joy sight-seeing and Norbert stayed and helped Harold build some greenhouses. One day Norbert even pitched in and helped me clean the house. Tommy was only three months old. I was still washing on the board and could hardly put one foot before the other. The day Norbert helped me clean the house, I fell across the bed so tired that I could hardly move. I was going to put on a clean dress and comb my hair. I can't imagine being too tired to do that now, but I was. I finally combed my hair, but just did not have the energy to change my dress.

I had put my coat on to go outside, when Norbert said, "Mother, you look like a little girl." And Ruth Joy said, "No wonder, she combed her hair." Then her hand flew to her mouth.

She was sorry for what she had said. I said, "I understand, honey, that's alright."

Well, the last four days they were there, we had fried apples for breakfast, fried apples for dinner, and fried apples for supper. When Ruth Joy got back to school, she sent me a thank you note and thanked me for the fried apples. I laughed to myself when I read her words.

I was reminded of the Israelites as they were fed by God in the desert. Because they had no way to provide for themselves, they had to depend on the Lord's care. Perhaps that is why it is more difficult for the wealthy to recognize their need of God.

God used the desert experience to strengthen the Israelites.

Moses said, "And He humbled thee, and suffered thee to hunger, and fed thee with manna which thou knewest not, neither did thy fathers know, that He might make thee know that man doth not live by bread alone, but by every word that proceedeth out of the mouth of the Lord doth man live." Deut. 8:3.

If we are to have true life we need not only to be fed physically, we need a living relationship with our God through Jesus Christ. Jesus said, "I am the bread which came down from heaven." "Verily, verily, I say unto you, He that believeth on me hath everlasting life. I am that bread of life." John 6:41b, 47-48.

This was the faith that Betty had. She had been in need and the Lord had provided in such a gracious way, but more than that, her faith was established in her Savior, Jesus Christ. He had given her the greatest gift of all. Jesus came to this earth from His glorious heavenly home. He came to give His life as a sacrifice for our sins, so that we might be forgiven and be saved. By her faith in Jesus Christ, Betty had received the best gift of all—eternal life. That walk of faith began the moment she placed her trust in Jesus Christ as Lord and Savior. That walk of faith continues as she keeps her hand in Jesus' hand.

Praise God, we have a Savior who never gives up on us and never lets us go.

CHAPTER 13

God's Providence and Man's Frailty

"Boast not thyself of tomorrow, for thou knoweth not what a day may bring forth." Proverbs 27:1

Just before Larry, my oldest boy, graduated from high school, he joined the Marine Reserve. He graduated in June, 1951. The Korean War was going on, and in August they called in his outfit. He did not even go to boot camp but was sent directly to Camp Lejune. In January, they were ordered to the front lines and were in the midst of the fighting.

When he told us that he was ordered overseas, the Lord gave me peace because I somehow knew the Lord would bring him back.

It really tore Harold to pieces. Later, I think Larry thought that his Daddy cared more than I did. After he left I would think about how so many of our boys had frozen to death that first year, because they were not prepared for the severe Korean weather. I prayed so much for the Lord to keep him warm. I cried a lot those days, but the Lord understood a mother's heart and He always restored my peace.

Larry was there quite a long time. He was promoted to corporal and carried the walkie-talkie so he could report back to headquarters. One day the men were ordered to man the machine guns for battle. Larry said that usually you would hear the enemies' bullets coming, but that day they did not hear anything.

Suddenly one bullet cut across Larry's chest, cutting the walkie-talkie off. The same bullet then entered the man next to him, and killed him. The young man was due to go home the next day.

A bullet then hit Larry in the leg and another one hit him in the arm. He managed to call on the walkie-talkie for help. The medics came and carried the wounded back to camp.

At that time they didn't have any x-ray machines in his camp. Some of the boys had been faking injuries to go home. So the doctor assumed that Larry's injuries were not serious and ordered him to go take a shower. He could not get up, but he scooted to the shower and took one. Later, when a ship came in with an x-ray machine on it, the doctor saw that Larry's leg was truly fractured, so he sent him to get medical care.

I was by myself when the telegram came from the War Department. Before I opened it, I got on my knees and asked the Lord, "Whatever this telegram says, may your name be glorified in some way through it." When I opened the telegram, all it said was, "Your son was wounded in battle." There were no details at all.

God's peace descended on me in a wonderful way. People would come to see me to console me, and they could not understand my calmness. Surely that verse, "Thou wilt keep him in perfect peace, whose mind is stayed on Thee, because he trusteth in Thee," Isa. 26:3, proved true to me.

After several weeks, I finally received a letter from Larry telling me about his injury. Much later the army sent a telegram saying that his arm and leg had been wounded.

Later my neighbors had to go through a real tragedy with their son. He told me it helped them so much to remember how the Lord had given me peace at that time. I think any experience that we may go through not only strengthens us, but also prepares us to help others.

When Larry was discharged, he took his mustering out pay to buy a car for himself and a beautiful Westinghouse refrigerator for me, the first one I ever owned. It was still running thirty years later when I sold it to a neighbor.

****

When Mark was nine, he came into the house, lifted the stove lid and put in an old electric light bulb. I yelled at him.
"What are you doing? Don't do that!" but the bulb was already in. He said, "It won't hurt anything." He kept waiting to hear it explode. After awhile, he lifted the lid to see what was happening. When the air hit it, it exploded! A piece of glass flew in Mark's eye making a deep cut in it. He screamed out in pain and doubled over. We were by ourselves, so first I had him kneel with me in prayer, asking the Lord what to do. We had no phone, so I went to my nearest neighbor who came back with me and took us to the doctor. He immediately sent us to the hospital. Mark had to

have two operations to repair the damage.

We did not have any medical insurance, and when he had to have the second operation, the administrator of the hospital came and told me that we would not have to pay for the second hospitalization. The Lord was so good since I had not said a word about the bill to her. When we brought Mark home from the hospital, Larry, who was working at the time, got a large television for the children. It was our first television. Mark can still only see a little light through that eye. Sometimes the price of disobedience is high.

It had turned cold while Mark was in the hospital and all three of the little ones needed coats. So when I got Mark out of the hospital, I took my grocery money and bought coats for them.

I had no idea where the food would come from, but the Lord would work it out somehow. At that time, Bobby was dating a young lady named Gertrude. She lived on a farm. That very night, her mother asked him if we could use some milk because her cows were giving more than she could use. Bobby said he was sure I could.

The Lord saw us through that time like He always does. I always knew when Bobby had a date with her, because there would be a gallon of milk for me the next day. Later they got married.

Gertrude and I had many precious times together, and she was in my Sunday School class for a while.

Mark was quite an adventurous little boy and therefore had many accidents. One evening he was running through the yard after dark and ran into an old airplane that needed repair.

Harold had brought it home to recover it and it was sitting in the yard. That time he cut a place in his right temple. It was bleeding terribly. Again, we were alone. After pressing a towel hard against the cut, I had prayer with him. The day before, I had picked up a first aid book and had read what to do. Surely the Lord was preparing me for this. Again, I ran over to get my neighbor. I do not know what I would have done without Floyd Bates. Though he had a new car, he let a friend use it to take me to the doctor, blood and all. All my neighbors were surely nice to me.

The doctor had to sew the artery together. I would talk to Mark about Jesus, telling him that He could help. And thank the Lord, they did stop the bleeding in time. The doctor and my neighbor just looked at me when I talked to Mark about the Lord while the doctor was treating him.

****

When Larry got back from the service, he had a few odd jobs and then went to work for Virginia Electric Power Company. Some time later, after he was married and had children, he was up on a pole doing some work. Without warning the belt he had around his waist broke and he fell ninety feet. A telephone wire was the only thing that broke his fall. He said as he was falling that the verse, "Boast not thyself of tomorrow, for thou knoweth not what a day may bring forth," kept coming into his mind. As he lay there, he had to tell the men around him what to do. They were in a state of shock. His back was broken and he was in a cast for quite a while.

Gertrude's brother, Franklin, who also worked for the power company, was killed one day when he was up in a bucket working on a transformer which exploded. He was such a likeable young man.

At one time he had been in one of my classes. I know he knew the way of salvation, however, I do not know if he made a public profession of faith, but still we do not know the heart. Only God knows.

I know one day I had given the members of the class a paper with a heart drawn on it, with various sins written inside of the heart. I told them to take it home and that night to go over each sin. If they were guilty of any of the sins, they were to confess it. The next night he came to me grinning and said, "Mrs. Fitzgerald, I didn't get any sleep last night. I was so busy confessing my sins." He was around fifteen years old at the time and he was teasing me. I really felt drawn to him. Lots of times we do not realize how important it is that the ones in our class know the truth. We need to make the most of every opportunity, since we never know how long any of us have in this life. He was only in his thirties when he was killed.

Since life is short and death may come unexpectedly, we need to take every opportunity that God provides to witness to others about Jesus Christ. Certainly there will be some who reject what we have to say, but we can be sure that God has been working in some people's hearts long before we bear witness to the truth.

The Father may be drawing that person to Him. And He may lead you or me to tell him that Jesus died to save him from his sins.

After talking with the Samaritan woman at the well, Jesus said to His disciples, "Say not ye, There are yet four months and then cometh the harvest? Behold I say unto you, Lift up your eyes and look on the fields; for they are white already to harvest." John 4:35. Whether we are sowing or reaping, the main thing is that we are faithful to our Lord. If we are working in the fields, leading people to Jesus Christ, we can be sure that we will have great joy over those who are being saved, or those being led into deeper walk with our Lord.

CHAPTER 14

Trust and Obey

"Trust in the Lord with all your heart and lean not unto thine own understanding; in all thy ways acknowledge Him and He shall direct thy paths." Proverbs 3:5-6

It is true that accepting Jesus Christ as Lord and Savior means a new birth. As the Holy Spirit comes to dwell within us, we are born anew. By God's grace we are given a new spiritual life, an eternal life to be lived in fellowship with our Heavenly Father through Jesus Christ, His Son. But the new birth is just the beginning. It is God's intention that we grow as Christians.

It is God's desire that we yield our lives to Him. Service to God is not a burden—but a glorious privilege. As Proverbs 3:5-6 says, we are to trust the Lord with *all* our heart, and we are to acknowledge Him in *all* our ways. When we do this, God promises that He will direct our paths. Remember the hymn—

"When we walk with the Lord
In the light of His word
What a glory He sheds on our way!
Let us do His good will,
He abides with us still,
And with all who will trust and obey.
Trust and obey, for there's no other way
To be happy in Jesus, But to trust and obey."

Shortly after I joined Immanuel Baptist Church, my Sunday School teacher asked me if I would give my testimony. I told her I would. Already, I was forming in my mind that I would use the verse, "I can do all things through Christ who strengtheneth me."

Philippians 4:13, and I had prepared what I was going to say.

However, in the middle of the night, the Lord woke me and said, "That is not your testimony. Your testimony is, "God is our refuge and strength, a very present help in time of trouble." Psalms 46:1.

As I shared my testimony, I told them how the Lord had led me to that church. He placed me in that church because He knew what I needed for my spiritual growth. When there was something I could not understand, I would pray to the Lord. Wonderfully, the next Sunday, the preacher would say, "The Lord won't let me preach the sermon I prepared, but I must preach on this, so pray for me." The Lord then used the sermon to open my eyes and answer my questions. As I shared my testimony, the preacher was listening. I was perfectly calm while I was talking; but when I got back to my seat, I was shaking all over. I think it is important for a Christian to share his testimony. Satan is the one who puts fear in our heart, and if we give in to that fear it becomes harder and harder to speak openly of our faith.

The Lord began to lead me out. I had a neighbor who belonged to a Presbyterian Circle, and when their teacher was sick, she asked me to teach. The Lord had a way of putting me with people who always had so much more than I did, but He did not let me be self-conscious. I saw people only two ways—they were either saved or lost-nowhere in between. I taught the circle once a month, and so many precious ones came to the Lord. Then the devil got in. Unknown to me, there had been some opposition to my teaching. I really felt the Lord had given me the messages there. Sometimes, though, when the word of God is taught plainly, it brings division. So to eliminate the problem—me, they passed a rule that you had to be a member of the church to teach.

No one wanted to confront me, so they waited until the teacher who had been sick returned to tell me. However, they did call on me to pray that evening. I know the Lord must have prayed through me that night. He protected me from hurt and gave me the words to speak. (See Matthew 10:17-20) Being a new Christian at the time, I know that the Lord taught me many lessons through this.

****

After fourteen years of preparation at Immanuel Baptist Church, the Lord began to lead me to move my membership to Kingsland Baptist Church where I had more opportunities for service. I had often visited Kingsland Baptist Church, a little church across the road, because Immanuel was so far away. In the summer time, I had taught in their Vacation Bible School, and on Sunday evenings, I had worked with their young people in Baptist Training Union. It was a small church that had been in the same building for fifty years.

One day, two of the deacons came to my house and invited me to their revival. I went and enjoyed myself very much. I felt the Spirit there that night. After that, the Lord began to deal with me about changing my membership. At first I could not believe that it was the Lord leading me there. At the time I was going to Immanuel Baptist Church, the pastor, Brother Seume, was preaching the Word clearly and I was perfectly happy. When I was a new member, and Pastor Sampson was there, they had voted to withdraw from the Southern Baptist Convention. I did not know what it was all about, having come from a different background.

Although they did not say it in so many words, you got the impression that they thought Southern Baptists compromised. I thought, "How can the Lord be leading me to Kingsland Baptist Church, a Southern Baptist Church?" But the Lord let me know what He called "clean", I was not to call "unclean".

The feeling was so strong that I finally told the Lord that if He wanted me to join that church to make it impossible for me to get to mine. It was Easter Sunday and Harold took me to a Sunrise Service. We got back too late to go to my church, so the children and I went to this one. They were without a pastor at the time. All during the sermon, I just knew that I had misunderstood the Lord. He surely did not want me there, but the Lord spoke to me through the words of the preacher. He quoted a verse that had led a missionary to the mission field.

Just as the Lord had led her to a foreign mission field, I felt He was calling me to a mission field, there at Kingsland Baptist Church. When the invitation was given, I went forward to join the church.

My neighbor took us home, and said, "Mrs. Fitzgerald, I am glad you joined us today." I replied, "I sure hope I did the right thing." Jimmy said, "Mama, what have you done? Now we can't go back to our church." When I got home I went to the bedroom and began to talk with the Lord. I just knew my children would have teachers that were not born-again, but the Lord gave me the verse, Genesis 50:21, to reassure me. The part that stood out was, "I will nourish you and your little ones."

One of the classes I had at Kingsland was a young married ladies' class. That class stayed in a state of revival. They went visiting, came to a home Bible study at my home, and grew by leaps and bounds.

They put me on the nominating committee. They were also looking for a president for the Women's Missionary Union, but could not get anyone to take it. One night at home the Lord let me know He wanted me to take it. I did not even know what a W. M. U." was! The next night when we were meeting, everyone looked at me and asked me to take it. I did, because the Lord had told me to do so and I held that position for four years. I prayed and the Lord gave me ten guidelines to follow. I had much opposition, but somehow the Lord worked it out.

As president of the W. M. U., I initiated a special week on missions. I did this because I had seen the benefits of missions week at Immanuel Baptist Church. It was held once a year. I called the Foreign Mission Board and asked for missionaries to speak. At first only three ladies and maybe one man attended.

As time went by, attendance increased. The Lord honored our faithfulness and the church really went forward with missions.

When Jimmy Russ came as our pastor, he too had to go through much opposition, but then the people began to get saved. His heart was in missions and the Lord used him greatly in getting the missionary program off to a good start.

The ones you would have thought were the spiritual leaders of the church finally left. They gave the most trouble.

Jimmy stayed for seven years then resigned. Right before he left, we had a revival. The evangelist was Rev. Frank LaPierre.

He really went deep into the word. The Pastor Search Committee had not yet found a pastor. The morning of the last meeting, while sitting on the front row, the Lord spoke to me and told me that he was the man. I did not know what to do, so when I went out the door, I told one of the deacons.

Later they called him. Several years ago I asked Rev. LaPierre when they had interviewed him. He said they talked with him just before he got on the plane. He told me that when he got home, both he and his wife got on their knees and told the Lord if that was the church for him that the church would call him.

He stayed with Kingsland Baptist Church for about twenty years until his retirement.

While I was at Kingsland, the church grew spiritually and

numerically. I saw that church build a new sanctuary with additional classrooms under the leadership of Pastor Russ and build a large educational building under the leadership of Pastor Frank LaPierre. The original church has been torn down and they now have two large parking lots. Brother Frank said to me one day, "Why should we, who love the Lord, leave the Southern Baptist Convention, which was founded on the Word, and turn it over to the liberals? No, we will stay and fight." That gave me a different view of the church. All through the years the Lord has kept me with Southern Baptist churches.

About fourteen years after joining Kingsland, the Lord began to deal with me about giving up my Sunday School class. He led me to this decision in several ways. He put me through a busy year which kept me away from church. Before that I had never missed a service. We had bought some land by the Coan River and we would go down to work on a cabin. Harold had a job at that time that gave him three days work, then three days off. When his days off would fall on week-ends, I would put my foot down.

I felt that I had to be at church to teach my class. It really got to be a sore spot, because he resented the church anyway.

Then I had an accident, and was unable to go for awhile. The Lord kept speaking about letting go and letting God.

Finally, I talked to Brother Frank about it. I had been praying for the Lord to lead me out any way He chose. When I told him everything involved, he said, "I wish sometimes that my leading was that clear." So, I gave up my class.

That week-end I told Harold if he wanted to stay over we could. I decided to go to church down there, so we left to work on our place at Coan River. When we got about ten miles down the road, he said, "I forgot something." When we went back home, he got his suit. That Sunday he went to church with me. I was surprised since he had never gone to either Immanuel or Kingsland Baptist churches with me.

At the age of 67, Harold built a small cabin, then later a house at Coan River. Even though we had no bath, the house looked nice and was comfortable. I would help him all that I could. I even helped put the shingles on the roof. He also dug a well by hand. He would go up and down a ladder carrying the dirt out.

When he struck water, he hardly got out of the well before the water rose. Until recently that well supplied our place and a place that Bobby built, but now Bobby has his own well.

Harold was a remarkable man in many ways. What he could have done if he had been open to the Lord, only God knows! I cried out to the Lord many times to make the Coan River a place like L'ABri for discouraged people to come and renew their strength and courage. Harold later sold it to Tommy, who sold it to Bobby and now Roger, Bobby's son, owns it. Roger is making a beautiful place out of it. It is not a L'Abri now, but in the future who knows?

The Holy Spirit, as I said, had led me to give up my Sunday School class. I did not really understand why completely, but I wanted to be obedient. Yet, when the superintendent of the Sunday School came to me and asked me to substitute for a teacher who would be away, I agreed to do it. But that Saturday night Lela, Mark's wife, called me. She told me that Mark had fallen off the roof and was in the hospital. We went over there and spent the night in the hospital. This prevented me from teaching the class. I sensed then that the Lord wanted full obedience.

He did not want me to teach Sunday School at all for a while. I loved the Lord, so I wanted to be obedient. Through obedience I have come to know the richness of Jesus' love. Jesus encourages us with these words, "If you obey my commands, you will remain in my love, just as I have obeyed my Father's commands and remain in His love. I have told you this so that my joy may be in you and that your joy may be complete." John 15:10-11

And as the hymn writer says—

> "But we never can prove the delights of His love
> Until all on the altar we lay;
> For the favor He shows, and the joy He bestows
> Are for them who will trust and obey.

I had always taught in Vacation Bible School. Harold had started taking Thursdays off, and for a change wanted to take us out. His mother and father were with us so I decided not to teach that summer. On Wednesday night, the lady who was teaching the class I generally taught, had someone call to ask if I would give the Bible lesson Thursday because she had lost her voice.

They told me I could go home right after the study. Thursday, at the breakfast table when I told Harold and his parents, I had to go to the church for about forty-five minutes, you would think I had dropped a bomb. From then on, he took all money away from me.

So when the church got ready to sell bonds, of course, I did not have any money to get one. I did not tell anyone about this until several years later. Pastor Russ thought that I just did not go along with selling bonds. I did not say anything then, but later when Harold wanted to sell some land, I would not sign unless he would let me buy a bond, which he did. Later when Harold needed a car, we were able to cash the bond and he got the car. The Lord always supplied our needs. When things like this happened it threw me more on the Lord and He never let me down.

I was His child and He took care of me. Truly He does supply all our needs according to His riches in glory by Christ Jesus. (Philippians 4:19)

It is truly overwhelming what the Lord has done for me. On one occasion the children were playing in the yard. It was way past supper time, but I let them continue playing. All I had in the house was a box of corn flakes. I was ironing and talking to the Lord. I remember saying, "Lord, even if you send in food, I am too tired to cook it." After a while my neighbor, Wilma, came over. Her children were playing with mine. She said, "I made some ice cream. If you come over, I will give you some." I told her I was so tired and just did not know if I could walk over there. She told me "Well, I am not bringing it over to you, because the last time I gave you some, you gave yours away." We talked and after awhile I said, " Well, I believe I will walk over for a few minutes, maybe I'll feel better." So, we gathered the children and went over.

When we arrived, her supper was still on the table. She said, "Oh, have you all eaten supper yet?" I replied, "No." So she put clean plates out and we sat down to one of the nicest meals I had eaten in a long time. We had ham, green beans, potatoes, sliced tomatoes, tall glasses of ice tea, and dessert of ice cream and cake. Afterwards, we sat on the porch and talked. I went home really renewed. Twenty years later, I shared with her how much that meal meant to us. She had no idea that we had no groceries at that time. The Lord is precious and He looks after His own. Praise His name!

Another day when I was working in the garden I became very discouraged. It was our twenty-fifth wedding anniversary.

Harold had said nothing, which was not unusual, because he always said that was one day he wanted to forget. I was having a "pity-party," feeling sorry for myself, when one of the children ran down with a package for me. When I opened it, there was a lovely set of silverware, the prettiest set I had ever had. Betty and Norbert had gotten it for me even though they did not have a set for themselves and were still in college on a tight budget.

It seems that when I am at my lowest point, the Lord moves someone to do something like that. We have a wonderful Lord!

Over the years the Lord has used some of my children to give and give. Then later when they are not able to help me, the Lord has used some of my other children.

All of my children are very precious. The Lord has been so good to me. If I would recount all the times and things the Lord has done for me, I would never finish this book.

Trust and Obey

Not a burden we bear,
Not a sorrow we share,
But our toil He doth richly repay;
Not a grief or a loss,
Not a frown or a cross,
But is blest if we trust and obey.

****

The Lord has always been so patient as He has led me in a deeper walk. I remember one of the times He helped me put my fears aside and place my trust in Him.

While I had a Bible class in Lillie's home, her sister, Blanche and her husband were building a brick home next door.

Although it was not finished, they lived in it. Her husband, Herbert, became ill. During the Bible study, I would look out and see Blanche hanging out her clothes. She had such a frown on her face. It was all I could do to make myself go to her and ask about her husband's illness. I was actually afraid of her.

The Lord started to deal with me about talking to him about the Lord. I walked the floor for several days trying to get my courage up. I asked my neighbor about him. She said, "At one time he was a Jehovah's Witness and they say, if you mention anything about the Lord, he will curse you." Well, that did not help, but I knew if I was to have any peace I would have to go.

He lived about a mile and a half from me. One day I started out walking to go there in fear and trembling. As I walked, I prayed, "Lord, I don't know what to say. Please speak through me." When I was almost there, I stopped and asked a girl to go with me for moral support. She was not even a Christian, but later became one. As we entered, Blanche was standing in the doorway by the bedroom. I do not know what I said. I only remember telling him how much the Lord loved him. He had tears in his eyes and she did too. Then we left.

He was sick for several months, but when he got better, he gathered his whole family and started to church. He and his family came regularly. Years later when he died, they remained faithful. David, his youngest son, is really serving the Lord and is the leader of the Royal Ambassadors. I saw him this summer for the first time since he was a little boy. Doris, David's sister, had a little one that the doctor said would never walk, but the Lord worked a miracle in her life.

Now Blanche and I are good friends. It's hard to imagine that at one time I was afraid of her. We laugh about that. I've often wondered what would have happened if I had disobeyed the Lord. We do not know what an act of obedience or an act of disobedience will bring about in far reaching results.

People, may we always be obedient in the simplest things!

> Then in fellowship sweet
> We will sit at His feet
> Or we'll walk by His side in the way
> What He says we will do,
> Where He sends we will go
> Never fear only trust and obey.
> Trust and obey for there's no other way
> To be happy in Jesus, but to trust and obey.

CHAPTER 15

Miracles of the Lord

"These things have I written unto you that believe on the name of the Son of God; that ye may know that ye have eternal life and that ye may believe on the name of the Son of God." 1 John 5:13

We had a visitation program once a week while I was at Kingsland Baptist Church. Because I loved visiting so much, almost every day I would finish my housework and go out visiting.

There is no greater joy than going to someone's home to talk to them about the Lord Jesus Christ. I walked for miles. Some of the people who did not visit began to say, "She ought to stay home and do her work, instead of going out with her Bible in her arms every day." I took it to the Lord in prayer and this is how He worked it out.

The Rescue Squad was looking for a temporary location while they were building their new station. So they bought the lot right next to me. They put a moble home there as their station.

The same people who had criticized me, worked there and they saw me work in my garden, put up a fence, cut grass and do my regular house work. I never heard them talking about it after that.

Lillie asked me to go visiting with her to see Doris, Blanche's daughter. She had just had a little one. The baby was born with a spinal birth defect. The doctor had told Doris that it would be better for the child if they left her in the institution as she would be unable to walk and mentally impaired.

As I walked out the door, I picked up a copy of *ANGEL UNAWARE* by Dale Evans, and took it with me. Our visit was not unusual. We sat and talked and I gave her the book. Soon after, she read the book and immediately she took her baby out of the institution and brought her home. She already had a little two year old girl named Sandi. Soon after she brought Stacie home, her husband deserted the family. So Doris got a job. Her mother kept the children, and somehow they managed.

Later, she met a nice man and they got married. Joel, her husband, loved the children from the start. He would sit for hours and massage Stacie' legs. As an infant she had to wear a body cast. Finally, with leg braces and crutches, she began to walk.

I did not hear from them for years. Then in 1981, I went to visit my son Jimmy in Atlanta. I learned that Doris had moved to Atlanta and we went to see her. Stacie was going to school then.

She still was on crutches and had braces, but she could walk.

Doris never treated one child above the other, so Stacie was pretty independent. She was able to dress herself and even did little things around the house. Doris and Joel had a little girl, her name was Jill, so now they had three daughters.

The radio station in Atlanta had a contest. The prize was a bicycle for the best letter expressing why they wanted one.

Sandi entered and wrote that she wanted a bicycle for her sister Stacie so she could ride with the other children. She won, and at the time I was there, the bicycle company was in the process of building a special bicycle that Stacie could ride. I did not see Stacie again until the summer of 1985. She was either fourteen or fifteen then, a beautiful girl, she smiled a lot, still wearing her braces and on crutches, but did not let it hinder her at all.

Doris called one day. They were in Richmond, and they were planning to go on a picnic at a lake not far from where I lived.

She asked if they could come by and visit me for awhile. I invited them to have lunch at my home. After lunch my grandchildren and I went with them to the lake. We had a wonderful time together.

When they left that night, all of their children asked if they could call me "grandma." I told them that they sure could.

I'll never forget when Stacie looked at me, smiled, and said, "I have a special reason for calling you grandma." Doris had told her many times about the book that I had taken her and how the Lord had used it to cause her to go take Stacie out of the institution. The Lord is so good to us!

****

One day, I heard a missionary tell about the time they were taking the gospel to some people. As they spoke, the people began to stone them and run them out of the village. A lady in the congregation spoke up and asked her if the stoning hurt her very much. She said, "You know, it should have, because we were bleeding, but it was just like the Lord held a pillow between me and the hurt." In my heart was the desire to experience the same protection from the Lord

That desire was satisfied one day when Harold and I were looking at some land that we had bought. While walking through the undergrowth, I stepped on a yellow jackets' nest and they immediately came out in force. I was running and crying. I lost my shoe and was stepping on holly leaves with bees all over me.

Harold was running after me, trying to knock the bees off, yelling, "Sit down! Sit down!" When I finally sat down he was beating the bees off and I was yelling. He said that if anyone had seen us, they would have thought that he was beating me up.

We had some rubbing alcohol in the camper so I rubbed that all over me, and the pain subsided.

I seemed to be alright, so Harold took me home. Then he went back for the weekend to clear some of the land. We lived about one hundred miles from the property. That morning right after he left, I began to swell and itch all over. It started up one side until it went all over me. I thought I would die. I would cry out to the Lord Jesus and He sent me peace for a while, but then the itching would start again. Each time I cried out to the Lord, he answered and truly it was as if He held a pillow between me and the pain.

When Harold got home that Sunday night, he saw the condition I was in. He took me to the doctor the first thing in the morning. I was a sight to behold. My clothes were half on because I was so swollen out of shape. The doctor gave me a shot; but one thing was certain, the Lord gave my answer — He did hold a pillow between me and the pain. Years later when I had my wreck, I really experienced it. God was with me all through the fourteen hours pinned in the car and in the hospital. I am so thankful for His comfort in the midst of pain.

We have a wonderful Lord, He does not take away the hard things but He goes through them with us. Just like the quiet in the eye of the hurricane, things can be all wrong all around us, but He keeps us in perfect peace.

****

We lived in the neighborhood on Willis road for twenty-seven years. Wilma still tells everybody that in all that time, we never argued. About fifteen years after we had all moved away, Iva Lee, Floyd's daughter, called and told me that her daddy was dying of cancer. She asked me if I would go see him. Although I lived over a hundred miles away and was sick, the Lord opened a way for me to go. I talked with Floyd who told me he was ready to die. I did not press him.

Later when a preacher came, Floyd knelt and asked the Lord to come into his heart. Floyd died a few days later. But since he placed his trust in Jesus, death had no hold on him. He went on home to be with his Lord.

As Paul says, "We are confident I say, and willing rather to be absent from the body, and present with the Lord." II Corinthians 5:8

As Christians we need have no fear of death. We can be sure of our salvation in Jesus Christ. What a wonderful miracle God works within us. Because of our faith in Christ we can be sure.

God's Word says, "And this is the record, that God hath given us eternal life, and His life is in His Son. He that hath the Son hath life and he that hath not the son of God hath not life.

These things have I written unto you that believe on the name of the Son of God; that ye may know that ye have *eternal life,* and that ye may believe on the name of the Son of God." I John 5:11-13

CHAPTER 16

God's Plan and Purpose

"For I know the thoughts that I think toward you, saith the Lord, thoughts of peace, and not of evil, to give you an expected end." Jeremiah 29:11

One day as I was cutting the grass, I accidentally pulled the mower over my foot. I reached down and began to feel my toes. When I got to the big toe, I saw the shoe was cut there and my big toe was just about cut off. My son, Mark, came over and took me to the hospital.

The doctor took stitches on my toe, but of course, I was off my foot for some time. Since the weather was extremely hot, lying there everyday was not very pleasant. So Nita, Larry's wife, took me to their house, which had an air conditioner. I was very comfortable there. She put me to bed, fixed me the nicest meals and carried me back and forth to the doctor. I will never forget her kindness to me. The Lord is always with you in trouble. With the eyes of faith you will see Him.

The Lord rescued me from fire one day. It was bitter cold with snow and ice everywhere. The children were all out somewhere and I was in the living room cleaning. I went to put some coal in the heater. I had on a cotton dress with an apron and a cotton smock over that. I took the edge of my apron to lift up the lid and my apron caught on fire! I panicked for a moment. As I stopped by the couch, I untied the apron. Then I quickly walked to the door and threw it out.

As I turned to go back in the house, I saw my couch was on fire! I tried every way I could to get the couch out the door, praying that the Lord would send someone in to help me. My son Jimmy came in right then, and we both tried to get the couch out, but we could not get it through the door. I told him that I was going after Floyd, my neighbor. So out the back door I ran to get Floyd.

However, to my surprise, when we got back, the couch was laying in the front yard all in flames. I asked Jimmy, "How did you get it out?" He said, "The Lord must have done it. When you opened the back door, the couch went up in flames, and I just picked it up and threw it out!" It is amazing what the Lord can do for His children.

That same day, Harold had a serious accident while giving a flying lesson. Harold survived without a scratch. Those two escapes from danger made me think seriously of how near death is to us at times. We could have both died that day and who would have cared for our children? I was so thankful for God's protecting hand.

****

Jimmy accepted the Lord when he was young. He loved to go to church. When we would have Youth Week at the church, he served in several ways. Once he led the prayer meeting. Another time he was the youth pastor. People would tell him, "If the Lord calls you to preach, don't turn Him down." However, during his senior year at high school, he began to drift away from the Lord. As soon as he graduated, he joined the Air Force, staying in for seven years.

While in the Air Force, he went through a very traumatic experience and felt he could not go on alone. So, he asked for leave and drove down to talk to Norbert, my son-in-law. Norbert talked and counseled with him most of the night, until he committed himself to the Lord. When Jimmy called me to tell me that he had come back to the Lord, he was in tears. They were tears of joy. He felt such peace in his heart.

The very next day when he went to church with them, he met Jeanette. From the beginning, he felt attracted to her. He asked Betty to invite her home for dinner, which she did. They began to date. After Jimmy got out of the service, he, too, went to Bryan College. While he was in college, Jimmy and Jeanette were married.

One day Jimmy said to me, "Mama, I have told the Lord if He wanted me to be a blue collar worker, I will be willing." I think he meant that he would be willing to do whatever the Lord required or asked of him. Isn't that really what God desires?

He wants us to give ourselves to Him so He can make something beautiful of our lives. God declares, "Behold, I make all things new." Rev. 21:5a There is not any area of our lives that

God does not want to cleanse and make new. For as we grow into mature Christians, we are being made into the likeness of Jesus Christ. That is God's will for us, if we will accept it. Saving faith means a life surrendered to the Lordship of Jesus Christ.

Abraham was called to give up his only son. Although God did not require his son's death, He wanted to know if Abraham loved Him as much as the heathen feared their gods. They offered their children trying to appease their gods.

We offer our lives out of a genuine love of God in gratitude for all He has done for us. Praise His name! He is a God who loves and cares for us.

****

Things had been getting pretty rough at home. It seemed that whenever I came into the room where Harold was, he could make me feel like dirt. I was getting to the place where all I could do was to cry out to the Lord. At that time, it seemed all I knew anymore was that Jesus had died on the cross for my sins and He was the Son of God. I could not seem to reach Him or hear His voice. But, I did cling to Jesus' sacrifice on the cross for me.

Christmas was drawing near and we were all trying to get ready for that. On Christmas Eve I got a call that my mother was in the hospital. She had had a heart attack and was not expected to live.

Christmas morning we opened our gifts. I could always tell Harold's feelings for me on Christmas. I felt such a coldness as I unwrapped my present from him. Inside the paper lay a small notebook. That morning, he took me around to see Lottie and Lillie for a little while, then he brought me home. As I watched him from the window, he went to the garage and got several large packages. He put them in the car and left. I knew those packages were for Gwen.

I stayed in the rest of the day by the telephone, in case they called about mother. It was a lonesome day. Several days after that, Gertrude, Bobby's wife, and I took Jimmy to the train station. He had been home for the holidays. While we were waiting for his train to leave, a little old lady got off. She looked so much like my mother, tears began to run down my cheeks.

My mother had always gotten off at this station whenever she came to visit me. It was more than I could take.

After Gertrude dropped me off, she went home and told Bobby, "I don't know what you all are going to do, but if it was my mother, I would see that she got to go see her mother." Bobby got on the phone and called the other children. Together they borrowed five hundred dollars and gave it to me for my birthday!

Bobby and Gertrude planned on taking me to Washington, D.C. to the airport, but that morning we had an ice storm and it was treacherous outside. So, he took me to the train station and I went to Washington by train. From Washington I flew to California to be with my mother.

In January we also learned that Harold's father was in the hospital, and not expected to live. So, when Bobby got home from the train station he took Harold to Louisville to see his father.

Because of the excitement of going, I had not even thought of calling anyone to let them know I was coming. I thank the Lord for going on before me to work things out. As we came into the San Francisco airport, the clouds were so beautiful. It looked like a winter wonderland. I could not help thinking, "I thought California was warm." About that time the pilot called out, "San Francisco is a balmy fifty-four degrees." While I had flown a lot, it was my first time on a large plane, flying above the clouds.

At the airport there were two large terminals. After claiming my baggage, I called the hospital and talked to my sister Catherine. It was at night so she told me to stay at the airport until she could find someone to come for me. Catherine got in touch with my nephew, Dan, who lived in San Francisco. I told her that I would be in front of the restaurant, but did not say which terminal. I waited and waited.

Finally, it came over the loudspeaker for me to come to the desk. They told me to take a certain passage which led me to the other terminal. So I had to carry all of my baggage. I knew that next time I would wait until someone came for me before claiming my bags. Finally, we found each other and went to the hospital. In the meanwhile, Catherine had rented one of the nurse's rooms for me. Since it was so late, I waited until morning to see Mama.

The next morning, when we went to see her, Catherine went in first to tell her I was there, so she would not be so shocked. When I saw my mother, she said, "Josephine, I have been praying I could see you. I thought maybe I could send you the money to come on, but I was afraid I might need it for my expenses."

I was praying on one end, and mama was praying on the other

end and God worked it out. I had prayed that the Lord would send a Spirit-filled person to go to my people and He sent me! It surely humbles you when something like that happens. As you know, apart from Him we are nothing. He is wonderful!

Mama was in the hospital two weeks longer. But after the first week, the doctor told us he thought she would live. When we went to tell Mama the good news, she did not think it was "good news" at all. You see, she was ready to go. She had been thinking about Heaven and all the loved ones who had gone before and she was disappointed she had to live. We could not help but laugh at her and the way she expressed herself. Catherine had to go back to Atlanta, but I stayed until Mama went home to my sister Louise's house in Concord.

While Mama was in the hospital, I prayed for my people.

Even though I knew that Mama was saved, I did not know how the others stood before the Lord. Catherine had gotten me a radio and all week I listened to a program coming from Mesa, Arizona.

The evangelist was preaching on the fifteenth chapter of John.

Jesus says, "I am the vine, ye are the branches." So, I knew all I had to do was to abide in Him. We had a good time those two weeks. I visited several of my nieces and nephews and enjoyed getting to know their families. Almost every day Louise would take me to a Goodwill Store which had nice clothes. I called it "my favorite department store".

A few days before I left, Ray, my brother-in-law, asked me what I believed. Everyone gathered around and I shared my beliefs with them, beginning with Jesus dying on the cross for my sins to the Second Coming! I was so thankful that the Lord Jesus had given me that opportunity. Years later just before Ray died, he told Louise to write and tell me he was alright—he knew the Lord. We need to be faithful in our witness, knowing the Bible says, "Therefore, my beloved brethren, be ye steadfast, unmoveable, always abounding in the work of the Lord, for as much as ye know that your labor is not in vain in the Lord." I Corinthians 15:58

When my visit was over, I redeemed my airplane ticket and caught the train to Kentucky. I stayed there a month and helped some with my father-in-law, who was still in the hospital. I stayed with Opal part of the time and then with Betty.

Jimmy came down while I was there. He said, "Mama, you are entirely different when you are not with Daddy." As I thought about that, I realized that I could just be myself when Harold was not around. Somehow in his presence, fear would creep in. In the same way Harold's friends saw him differently. They saw him as a gentle man, a side I rarely saw. We surely did not help each other's personality a bit. God had to do a lot of work in both of our lives.

While I was in Kentucky, Tommy, who was sixteen at the time, started calling me to find out when I was coming home. Tommy later told me that his Daddy got him to call me. I had left Richmond on the first of January and arrived home on the sixth of March. I took a bus to Virginia and when I arrived, no one was there to meet me. So, after waiting awhile, I caught another bus home. I arrived with one dollar in my pocket. The paper boy knocked on the door and took that.

For a while our marriage was much better. I believe Harold had thought I had left him forever. I even believe he may have missed me!

****

My youngest son, Tommy, married when he was twenty-three years old. Brenda, his wife, was a lovely girl. A little while after they were married, he joined the Army. He was later stationed in Germany and Brenda went to be with him, after he got settled.

Once while Tommy was on leave from Germany, he went to visit an old friend of his named Nick. Nick had recently given his life over to Jesus Christ. Nick and Tommy stayed up until about two o'clock in the morning talking about Jesus Christ and His plan of salvation. That night Tommy recommitted his life to Jesus Christ. The next morning he told me what had happened. I was so happy. What's more, we later found out that some of their neighbors in Germany had been witnessing to Brenda, his wife. She accepted Jesus Christ as Lord and Savior about the same time that Tommy had rededicated his life to Christ. God has a plan and a purpose for each life. It's only as we yield to His leading and follow in His way, that we see the wonderful beauty of how all the pieces fit together. On the other hand, if we do not submit to God's plan, we can miss out on some wonderful things that God has in store for us.

"For we are His workmanship, created in Christ Jesus unto good works, which God has before ordained that we should walk in them." Ephesians 2:10

CHAPTER 17

I Will Never Leave Thee

"Let your conversation be without covetousness; and be content with such things as ye have: for He hath said, I will never leave Thee, nor forsake Thee." Hebrews 13:5

The same day I was rejoicing over Tommy's experience with the Lord, I felt a sense of foreboding all day. Soon my joy was to be mixed with deep sorrow. About five P. M. I got a phone call from June, my oldest daughter, telling me that she had killed Harry, her husband. At first I just could not believe it.

But as we talked, I came to believe it was true. She had killed him. Her voice was that of a little girl. I knew that she must have been in shock.

Once while we were talking she went to see if Harry was really dead. While she was away from the phone, her little grandson who was there got on the phone, and said, "Grandpa, Mama shot Papa, bang, bang, he fall down." He thought it was a game.

I knew she needed help then, but we were eight hours away.

I told her to find her Bible and read some, and we would be there as soon as possible. She said, "Mama, I've done something against God." Her daddy told her to take some aspirin and wait until we could get there. She lived in South Carolina and we lived in Virginia. We made plans and got things together quickly. Rodney, their youngest son, was visiting us at the time. So we took him back with us. When June first called, it seemed that I just could not face it, I felt all torn apart. But as I turned to the Lord, He restored my peace. Truly when we are called upon to go through deep waters, He is there beside us to carry us through. He gave me that peace that passest all understanding. We have a wonderful Lord!

Mark had called Jimmy and Jeanette in Atlanta and they were already at the police station when we arrived. They had been looking everywhere for June, but no one knew about her. Finally we found out that she had killed herself.

When we went to the sheriff's house, he told us the story.

He was her next-door neighbor and thought so much of her. They had talked the day before. After she called us, she called there and told his wife what she had done. The sheriff was not home then, but went over as soon as he got home. When he arrived, June told him that she was making pickles when Harry came in.

He told her to pack her bags, and get out because he was bringing his mistress to live there. She opened the drawer, got the gun, and killed him. Whether he really was having an affair with another woman, I do not know. I do know he made her believe he was.

While the sheriff was calling someone, she made a dive for the gun. He tried to get it from her. But she quickly pulled the trigger and killed herself right in front of his eyes. It was such a tragic scene.

Eric, her oldest son, had gone to the beach that day to spend the week-end. Since he did not know anything about the shootings, Larry and Nita stayed at Eric's home to wait for them to get back. We went to a motel. The people at the motel were so nice to us. They gave us a private place where we could make coffee, and did all they could for us. All the family came down.

After June and Harry were placed in their coffins, I went to the funeral home to stay. As I looked at her, I thought to myself, "Honey, you look so peaceful, now, you can rest." Immediately I heard a voice say, "How can you say that when you know what she did?" Right after that, another inward voice said, "You leave her alone, she is my child."

Then I began to go back over June's life. She had seen the Lord work in my life over and over. I had talked to her about the Lord. But before my conversion, she had seen her Daddy and me go out to parties and drink. She could not wait until she was old enough to go out. Just as she turned sixteen, I was saved and told her all those worldly things were wrong. I suppose the change was confusing to her. She was a girl that was really lonely on the inside, but outwardly, she was the life of the party. She naturally drew people to herself.

One time when Harry was in Germany, June and her two boys went to a revival with me. During the invitation, I felt led to go to her and ask her if she wanted to be saved. She said, "This time if I go forward, I have to mean it." Not only did she go forward, but both of her boys and Tommy, my youngest son, went down that night. Later June, Tommy, and Scott were baptized, but Eric was sick.

When she went to Germany to join Harry, she started going to church. Then she got pregnant again and was terribly sick.

Later when Rodney was born, he was so sick that she stopped attending church. Even when they returned to the States, she did not go back to church. By not being involved in a church, she really missed the nurture that we all need as Christians. Just as babies are born into families, when we are born again as Christians, we need that fellowship of believers, the church, to help us grow up into mature Christians. Some say belonging to a church is not important. But in Ephesians 5:25, the Bible says, "Christ loved the church, and gave Himself for it." If Jesus Christ loved the church and made His sacrifice for it, then we as followers of Jesus should have a love and devotion to the church, too.

Later June had an opportunity to take a beauty course and go forward with that. While deciding what to do, she had to go to the hospital. She took her Bible and the beauty book to the hospital and told me that she had to decide between the two. I do not know what was involved there, but she laid down her Bible and picked up the beauty work. After the course, she went on first to be an apprentice. Later she owned a beauty shop with several girls under her. She prospered in her work. But her decision hurt her growth as a Christian. In choosing something good that she wanted for herself, she missed God's best. All through life we have choices to make. When we go our own way without seeking God's direction, we really miss God's blessings and closeness.

June had always wanted a large house with columns in front.

Since Harry and June were doing well financially, they began building their home. She fashioned it after the home in "Gone with The Wind." She even named it Tara Hall and that house meant everything to her.

I had seen signs of deep tragedy in her life. Sometimes I wonder if I could have done more to help turn things around.

Only the month before, June had told us that Harry had been running around on her and that he had threatened to throw her out of her beautiful home and bring the other woman there to live. I remembered her words. She said, "Mama, if he does, I will kill him." Then, I did not believe she really would. I thought they were merely threatening words. Now I know better.

Two years earlier we had visited her and she was talking about suicide then. But we went to a large rally at Columbia Bible College. When it was over she said, "I know what I have to do now." I think she really tried again to draw closer to Jesus.

She started reading her Bible everyday, just drinking it in. She would call me up long distance and ask me to pray for various ones who had needs. She was faithful in this way for over a year. But I am sorry to say that someone brought an Ouija Board into the home and they began to play with it. Little by little, she did not call as much for prayer requests. I believe that Satan was attempting to draw her away from her true devotion to Jesus Christ.

After the funeral, I looked all over for her Bible. She had always kept it by her bed. I finally found it in the upstairs bookcase that reached to the ceiling. It was pushed back on top of the top shelf of books. I do not know if Harry hid it or if she put it there.

Through all of this, the Lord still comforted me and gave me an understanding that my daughter was with the Lord. Do you know, she is still just as alive to me now? I never think of her as dead. Still, I am sorry that she did not allow Jesus Christ to carry her through the trials of this life. I know her sins were great, but I believe she really had trusted Jesus as her Savior earlier in her life. I believe that Jesus was faithful to save her.

She had a tragic life, but it did not have to be that way.

Even though she had accepted Jesus Christ, she let the things of this world have priority. Like the seeds that fell among the thorns in the parable of the sower, the cares of this world and the deceitfulness of riches choked out the Word and her life did not bear fruit as God intended. (Matthew 13:22)

If only June had trusted her life to Jesus Christ in all of her troubles. When we become a Christian that is just the beginning. As Christians we are not exempt from trials and struggles.

Jesus said, "These things I have spoken unto you, that in me ye might have peace. In the world ye shall have tribulation: but be of good cheer; I have overcome the world." (John 16:33) It is only Jesus who can give us true peace in this world.

How can we attain this peace in Christ Jesus? Paul says, "Do not be anxious about anything." (Phil 4:6a N.I.V.) In today's world we may think that is impossible, but Paul goes on to tell us how we may open up our lives to the peace that only Jesus Christ can give. Paul continues, "but in everything by prayer and petition, with thanksgiving, present your request to God. And the peace of God, which transcends all understanding, will guard your hearts and your minds in Christ Jesus." (Phil. 4:6b-7 N.I.V.)

If June had had that deep life with her Lord Jesus, she would have never done what she did. It is never the will of God that we take matters into our own hands and kill someone else that has brought pain into our lives. Nor is it God's will that we take our own life. He has given us life. He wants to give us an abundant life in Jesus (John 10:10). God may allow troubles and trials in our life in order to perfect our faith. In fact the Bible says that we should be joyful amidst trials. "My brethren, count it all joy when ye fall into divers temptations; knowing this, that the trying of your faith worketh patience.

But let patience have her perfect work, that ye may be perfect and entire, wanting nothing." (James 1:2-4)

It is our Father's will that we lack nothing. If we seem to be lacking in some area we need to pray to our Heavenly Father.

We need the life line of prayer to sustain our Christian life. We need to abide in Jesus Christ, then He can see us through anything.

In a wonderful pamphlet entitled "Committal" by James H. McConkey, he says, "Children of God, is not the truth very plain here? And does it not convict our hearts? There was a time in your life when you were sorely burdened in the effort to keep the rarest jewel in existence, that of your own soul. After years of self-effort, self-righteousness, and agonizing struggle you gave up the effort and simply and trustfully threw yourself upon Jesus Christ looking to Him in helpless trust to keep that which you have committed to Him. Wherefore, for years you have been at rest concerning the keeping of this precious jewel of your own soul, for you know whom you have believed and are persuaded that He is able to keep that which is committed to Him. Yet though at peace concerning your soul's salvation, your life is burdened with anxious prayer about a host of other things. You are anxious about your business, your health, your loved ones, your future, your friends, your service and ministry for Him, and your numberless other interests. Has it never dawned upon you that just as you committed your soul to Jesus Christ so He would have you commit everything else to Him? Have you never learned that only a perfect committal will give you a perfect peace? Have you never seen that the Blessed Lord is lovingly and tenderly interested in every detail of your life, and would have you commit all to Him, even as you committed the keeping of your soul?

For care is linked with keeping. He who keeps the treasure bears the care. Thus if we try to keep our lives *we* bear the care. But if we commit them and all their interests to God *He* bears it. Yet how can God keep that which we do not commit? 'I know whom I have believed and am persuaded that He is able to keep.' — what? That which I keep myself? That which I insist upon carrying, managing and worrying over? Nay, 'THAT WHICH I HAVE COMMITTED UNTO HIM.' 'Casting all your care upon Him' is as true for us as, 'He careth for you,' is true of Him. Wherefore, beloved, is there anything in your life that has long been a haunting shadow of care, a burden of anxiety, a barrier between you and perfect peace? If so, then search your heart and see if this be not the explanation of it. Take it, and definitely, finally, and irrevocably commit it to God. How else can He possibly keep it? Is this not the secret of your failure? There is nothing wrong with the trust-building! You are sure of that.

HE ABIDETH FAITHFUL. It must be in your failure to commit, for He has never since the world began failed to keep that which has been committed to Him. Wherefore if there be lack of perfect peace in your life hasten to make that perfect committal which will permit a perfect Christ to prove His perfect keeping."

I pray that as Christians, we will commit our whole lives to Jesus. We will then know true peace and what is more, maybe we can help a brother or sister in Christ who is struggling along the way. Oh, how I wish June had known the keeping power of Jesus Christ. I wish she had claimed God's promise, "I will never leave thee nor forsake thee." (Hebrews 13:5b)

CHAPTER 18

God's Love Drives Out Fear

"The Lord is my light and my salvation: whom shall I fear? The Lord is the strength of my life: of whom shall I be afraid?" Psalm 27:1

When we got home, Harold began to have dizzy spells. He got so bad that we had to take him to the hospital. He had a near stroke and was in the hospital ten days. While he was in the hospital, I had difficulty getting back and forth to see him. So Tommy and Brenda bought me a Volkswagon and encouraged me to learn how to drive. I tried to learn to drive the Volkswagon, but I had trouble shifting gears. So later Harold bought a 1973 Ford Pinto and I finally learned to drive and passed my driver's test at the age of sixty seven.

About this time, we decided to move from our home on Willis Road. We sold it and bought a summer home near Three Lakes in Powhatan. We stayed with our son, Mark while we winterized the home at the lake.

Before we finally moved in permanently, we took Jeff, who was nine at the time, and went to Furth, Germany. We went to visit Tommy and Brenda. Tommy was still stationed in Germany at the time. Mark, Jeff's dad, paid Jeff's way. Tommy had modified a Volkswagon Bus into a camper and got a tent. We all started out on a beautiful camping trip. First, we went to Belgium for several days. Neil Painter and his family, some friends of ours, were stationed there. We went to a Billy Graham Crusade while there. Seven different nations were involved. It was wonderful.

From there we went into France, parked our camper and took a boat over into England, crossing the English Channel. We stayed overnight and had a bed and breakfast room for thirty-five dollars. We had a big breakfast served in the garden. Then we visited a castle and took a shuttle boat back to France. We visited Paris and went up and down the French coast staying at different camp grounds. We visited several castles, cathedrals, and enjoyed the lovely countryside.

Then we went back to Germany since Brenda had to work that week. We spent the night there and started out again. We went to Nuremberg and Munich, where we visited the place where the Olympics had been held when the athletes from Israel were killed.

The place was crowded, and Jeff got separated from us. So, finally we decided to go back to where we were all together last.

He, too, had gone back and was waiting for us. Praise the Lord, he was alright!

From there, we went into Austria, a beautiful country. Here we saw some more castles. Then we crossed over into Switzerland where we took a cable car to the top of a mountain where Heidi grew up with her Grandfather.

We also went to Humoz, Switzerland, where Francis and Edith Shaffer have L'Abri. We stopped at the chapel there. I stayed on the porch of the chapel and Harold stayed in the camper, while Tommy went to the house to see if anything was happening. That morning Harold and I had had some differences while Tommy was taking Brenda to work. Harold was really mad at me.

As I stood on that chapel porch, I was inwardly going through a spiritual battle. As much as I had leaned on the Lord and walked with Him, when Harold came home at night, I would freeze up. I had such a fear of how he would act. But, on that chapel porch I lost all fear of him. Being released from that fear really made a difference, because after that we got along better.

There were no programs at L'Abri that day, so we started back to Munich to meet Brenda who was coming in on a train. My family was beginning to complain because the drinks were so hot.

In Europe there was very little ice. So I began to pray for some ice. After we picked up Brenda, we went to Liechtenstein, then to the source of the Rhone River, and then to a castle in Austria. From there we went to the castle which Walt Disney used for a model for Disneyland's castle. While there, a storm came up and we all began to run down the mountain. People scattered everywhere looking for cover as hail began to fall the size of marbles. Harold later told someone that Jeff said, "I am sure glad Grandma did not pray for block ice!" However, Jeff said Harold made that one up.

Europe was beautiful and most of the countries were so clean.

I really enjoyed it.

When we got back, Mark had called the other children and had a fiftieth wedding anniversary party for us. It was good seeing all the children. Opal, Harold's sister, and Buck came down to surprise us. She really helped to put everything in order. The Lord knew how much she was needed.

Yes, we had been married for fifty years. I had some good memories. My children had been a blessing to me. On the other hand, I had felt many heartaches with Harold during those fifty years. But through it all, Jesus was faithful.

Suffering in this life can serve as a refiner's fire. Such was the case with me, because the suffering led me to a greater trust in God. I would not trade my walk with the Lord for anything or anybody. As I am writing this, the verse comes to mind, "It is good that I have been afflicted. Before I was afflicted I went astray." (Psalm 119:71a) How true that was in my life!

Still I hope that Harold and I would have a closeness and true affection. Early in my Christain life, God had promised that Harold would be saved and I still had that assurance. Now that my fear of him had been lifted, perhaps I could be more open to change in our relationship. God had taken away the fear and given me more love. "There is no fear in love; but perfect love casteth out fear." (1 John 4:18a)

CHAPTER 19

Let Him Have His Way With Thee

"Being confident of this very thing, that He which hath begun a good work in you will perform it until the day of Jesus Christ:" Philippians 1:6

We moved to our home in Powhatan in 1975. Jeff stayed with his daddy for a couple of years and then came out there to live with us. Although our house was small, we enjoyed it very much.

It's cathedral ceilings made it seem more spacious. It took a while to get used to the place, but after I met my neighbors, joined the Home Extension Club, and started to work in the Library, I began to enjoy it. We planted fruit trees and had a large garden the first summer. In my spare time I made bottle dolls. Our days were always busy.

Since we now had to drive to church, I was able to go to church only on Sunday mornings. We began taking some of the children in the neighborhood to church with us. Two of the girls went forward to accept Christ. We also took another neighbor and her children for awhile. No matter where you are, the Lord opens a way for His witness. Sometimes our witness begins just by being a good neighbor.

There was an older man, Reggie, who lived alone with his dog. He had emphysema and could hardly breathe. He would take walks and stop and visit with Harold and me. While Reggie was able, he came and shared meals with us. When he was confined to his bed, I would go down and clean up for him. Most of the neighbors shunned him.

One day Reggie was at my house when Rayna, Mark's girlfriend, was there for a visit. We sat in the yard and began to talk to him about the Lord. For a long time after we went into the house he sat there looking down pondering what we had said. Later, he told me he expected me to talk about the Lord because I was older and his mama used to read the Bible all the time. But when Rayna talked to him, it made an impression because she was young.

He was in the hospital when we moved away, but one day he called us long distance and talked a long time. A week later, when the man came to change his oxygen tank, he was dead. I do believe he asked the Lord into his heart that day Rayna witnessed to him. At least he heard.

We had not been in Powhatan very long until Harold had an operation. We learned that he had cancer of the colon. Harold rested a few months after his surgery. Then he started working on the house again. For two and one-half years he took some medicine at home. It must have been some kind of radium, because he had to break the bottles to get to the medicine. The doctor took him off of it, when he thought Harold had recovered.

Slowly but surely, Harold and I began to go to more places and enjoyed doing things together most of the time. We had a precious neighbor, Sigred, who was from Germany. Since she was a beautician, I would have her fix my hair. I know I talked to her from time to time. We talked about the Lord some, but I do not remember ever asking her if she was saved. I took her oldest daughter to church and she had accepted the Lord. However, shortly after her daughter's conversion, Sigred died of a heart attack. I wish I had given a clearer witness to her. I wish I had asked her if she knew Jesus Christ. We really do not know how long any of us will live. Oh, that we might be conscious of that fact, if our friends are not saved. Jesus said, "I am the way, the truth and the life, no man cometh unto the Father but by me." There is no other way, but by Jesus.

****

When June and Harry died, Rodney, their youngest son, was only sixteen years old. He had always been a sweet boy. He tried to get his mother to take him to church and sometimes she would take him. He went to live with Eric, his oldest brother, and Connie for awhile. Then at eighteen, he got his own apartment. When things were settled each of the boys got quite a bit of money. He had always lived a sheltered life. But when he received his inheritance, his friends multiplied. Money always draws the wrong kind of friends.

One day, he had gone to a party at someone's home and there

was some drinking. During the night, one of the boys decided for the three of them to go down to the dock. He knew a man that kept his boat there. So he thought they could take a ride and bring it back in the morning and no one would know about it. Rodney went along with them.

When they started back to shore, they could not get the boat started. Rather than get caught, they decided to jump overboard and swim back to land. Rodney was a good swimmer. He had learned to swim in the family's swimming pool in their backyard. He had even been a lifeguard at the lake. Still, on the way back, Rodney was taken with cramps. One of the boys tried to save him, but if he had not let go, he would have drowned too.

Rodney lost his life on Mother's Day, at the age of twenty, just four years after his parents' death. I can not help but believe that the Lord took him home because He knew Rodney would not have a chance here. I believe Rodney is with the Lord.

If only we as parents would realize our responsibility to our children, I believe we would be more careful how we live our own lives. It is true that each one of us is responsible for our own sins. But in a sense our sins are visited upon our children in many ways, mostly by the life we live before them. When they see us do something, they feel like it is alright for them to do the same thing. If we could only realize that apart from Christ they are headed to eternal damnation, we would know the most important thing in this life is to point them to Jesus Christ.

"Only one life, it will soon be past. Only what's done for Christ will last."

****

Harold always said that our house in Powhatan was temporary until he found a better place. He wanted more land, a spring, an old barn and a root cellar. He said he did not care if the house was old, since he could always fix it up. We would go out, tramp over land, always looking.

Every time we went in search of a new home, Mildred, my neighbor, would be upset because she did not want me to move. I told her she did not have to worry, as he never would find what he wanted. That same day we went to a real estate office in Nelson County, Virginia. When Harold told her what he wanted, she said, "I don't have anything now, but if I find something, I will let you know."

A couple of weeks later, she called to say that she had found a place to show us. Well, the tract of land was twenty acres. It was all overgrown except a little spot around the house. With no steps, you had to climb a hill to get to the house. First, she showed us an old chestnut barn. Then she took us up to see a spring, where water was piped down to the house by gravity. Then she said, "Let me show you the root cellar." I knew then he was going to buy the place as those were all the things he wanted.

We moved to Nelson County in March of 1980. The house was old. The upstairs had never been finished. When we moved in, he was most concerned about clearing the land. After installing a bathroom, fixing the kitchen and plumbing and wiring the utility room for the washer and dryer, most of the first two years were spent working on the outside.

Things were pretty rough. The house was cold, unless you sat around the stove. We found many snakes, wasps, big black flies, chipmunks, mice and rats. I remember climbing over many things piled on the back porch for a look at the mountains.

Later, when it was warmer, I loved to sit on the front porch looking at the mountains. Always the verse would come to me, "I will lift up mine eyes unto the hills, from whence cometh my help. My help cometh from the Lord, which made heaven and the earth." Psalm 121:1-2. Somehow, after that time of refreshing, I would come in to face the day with a little more courage and strength.

There was so much to do outside that there was not time for the house. Always, when I started to feel how unfair it was that Harold was not working on the house, the Lord would bring this verse to me, "Prepare thy work without, and make it fit for thyself in the field; and afterwards build thine house." Proverbs 24:27. When I would think of that verse I could not say anything. There were roads to repair; field after field to clear; chicken houses, barn and workshop to build; and trees to plant. I could go on and on.

It was a joy when we started the work on the house. But it was not easy. It seemed like things were always in a mess for so long. I am sure I could not have gone through this if I had not had my boot camp, back years ago, when we moved to the other old house. It seemed again that we worked from the time we got up until bed time. I would go as long as I could. Then I would be so exhausted that I would have to stay in bed for a couple of days. I will have to praise Harold for his stamina. He could always keep on going.

****

In the summer of 1980, Tommy, my youngest son, experienced a real time of testing. It seemed that he could find no rest for his soul. As is often the case, he first sought to find peace by a geographical move.

Right after Nicole, their second child, was born, Tommy decided to move to California. He took their older daughter Angie who was only four years old at the time. He stayed with my sister in California until he found a job. Then he told Brenda to sell all their belongings in Norfolk and to stay with us until he could find a place for them. Right before she was planning to go to meet him, he called to say that he had decided to come back to Virginia.

When he and Angie returned, they all stayed with us at our place in Nelson County. At this time, Tommy was going through some deep depression. We wondered if he was losing his mind because he was so changeable. When we questioned him, he always said it was a spiritual thing, he was like a man tossed to and fro with little foundation in the Bible. I would listen and then try to give him the scriptural basis for certain beliefs. I wanted to help him set his faith on a sure foundation. Sometimes, he would laugh at me. Other times he would show such hatred in his eyes toward me. I knew Satan really wanted to take control of his life. Satan works hard to keep a Christian from submitting his will to God's will. Satan does not want a Christian to bear fruit, so he does all he can to put doubt and temptation into the Christian's heart. To Simon Peter, one of Jesus' strongest disciples, Jesus said, "Simon, Simon, Satan has asked to sift you as wheat. But I have prayed for you, Simon, that your faith may not fail. And when you have turned back, strengthen your brothers." Luke 22:31-32 N.I.V. We know that Peter did deny Jesus Christ three times. But we also know that he repented with tears and later gave his life in service to Jesus Christ.

While Tommy was going through this time of testing, he took our little tractor and would spend hours everyday clearing the land. A man with a bush hog refused the job because he was afraid of ruining his equipment. We had to have the tractor fixed many times. However, it seemed that the hard work helped to lessen his anxiety. I do believe the Lord used this move, so he would have an outlet because I know it helped his reasoning.

Jimmy, who is a psychologist, said, "He is hurting on the inside and no one can get in to help him. He is lonely." I told him I knew the Lord could help him if only he would trust in Him. You would see Tommy really lean toward the Lord, then draw back completely.

Even though Harold had turned his heart away from the Lord, he too tried to straighten out Tommy's thinking. Tommy had a real spiritual battle. Thoughts of suicide troubled his mind.

One day, he was walking around the place and I fell in step with him and let him talk. He talked on and on. When we got where the cars were, I will never forget what he said, "Mama, Satan has taken away everything I ever had, until he tried to take away my childhood faith, but he couldn't touch that. I remember when I was a little boy, how I would lie under the apple tree and talk to God. And everything I asked Him then, has come to pass." From that point on he began to get better. All through this, Brenda stood by him. Very few women would have.

Tommy and Brenda lived with us from August until February. Then they both got a job and moved to a place of their own. While living there Stephanie, their third daughter, was born. Tommy tried to keep steady employment in Virginia, but for some reason there always seemed to be a problem. Finally he went to Atlanta to stay with his brother Jimmy for awhile. There in Atlanta, he got a good job and had many advancements. God gifted him in the construction trade and Tommy has always been a hard worker. After that crisis of faith in 1980, Tommy went on to work in Atlanta and in the Washington, D. C. area.

One day Tommy told me, "Mama, at times I hated you." I told him, "I know, I saw it in your eyes." Then he said, "Mama, I never really hated you, that wasn't me." I told him, "I knew that too." Satan really went after him with all his might. Was Satan afraid of what God had planned for his life once he really turned it over to Him?

Still there have been many struggles in his life. He has not found peace in his marriage, nor in his own personal life. I feel that the Lord is still dealing with him. The Bible tells us, "For whom the Lord loveth He chasteneth." Hebrews 12:6a. It is better to have the struggle than to have a heart so hard that it no longer feels conviction from the Holy Spirit.

I know that God still has a call on his life and what is impossible with man is possible with God. My prayer is that God will continue to work with him until He fulfills the vision He gave him one day. This I know—that Jesus loves him. I also know that Jesus wants what is best for him. Why do we, as God's children, so often desire to keep control over our own lives.

Should we not trust our Creator to know what is best for us and trust that out of His abundance He will provide all that we need?

I Peter 4:19 encourages us to commit our souls to Him, a faithful Creator. We can be sure that the God that keeps us in Jesus Christ neither slumbers, nor sleeps. He is always there. It is always best when we let God have His way in our lives, for He loves us with such a great love and guides us with magnificent wisdom. I know that when Tommy does yield himself to God's will for his life, he will know true rest and joy and peace.

With all my children I think of that verse, "Being confident of this very thing, that He which hath begun a good work in you, will perform it until the day of Jesus Christ." Philippians 1:6

Having seen Him begin a good work in all my children how can I doubt the outcome? There hath not lacked any good thing that He hath promised me, all came to pass—or will. I have already been able to see the beautiful committed life of my daughter, Betty. I may not live to see my boys in Christian service for Him, but I have no doubt that it will happen. Praise the Lord!

CHAPTER 20

God's Appropriate Time

"And I heard a voice from heaven saying unto me, Write, Blessed are the dead which die in the Lord from henceforth: Yea, saith the Spirit, that they may rest from their labours; and their works do follow them." Revelation 14:13

As we were fixing up our house in Nelson County, Harold said, "We have to look for a rug." So we went to town, but felt really discouraged at the prices and did not care for the choices. So we came home without one.

The next day, Martin, a friend of Harold's, came down with his wife. To see if we were interested, he said, "You know Sears is putting down new carpet in their music department. I guess they will throw away their old carpet." I said, "I surely wish they would throw it our way." Then he told us that he had already asked the man to save it for us. Not only did Sears give it to us, but they cut it to the size we needed! We still have that carpet all through the house, even on the stairs. It shows no sign of wear and we have a lot of company.

"Now unto Him that is able to do exceeding abundantly above all that we ask or think, according to the power that worketh in us, unto Him be glory in the church by Christ Jesus throughout all ages, world without end." Ephesians 3:20-21

In the spring of that first year, Betty came to visit during Easter break. She brought one of the boys from the Children's Home where she and Norbert worked and Jeff who had been living with them. She helped me put the finishing touches on the newly installed bathroom.

Since Jeff was to enter high school the next year, he asked to stay with us and go to High School. Sure enough, Mark, his daddy, talked to Harold, and Jeff moved in that summer. The Lord revealed to me that if I had the right attitude toward him, things would be alright. After all, I was not any younger and did not know if I could take on a teenager or not. But he stayed with us eight years after that summer and having him proved to be a blessing to me.

Norbert and Betty began to come down for their vacations and always Norbert would start working on something to make the home safer for us. He rebuilt our stairs inside our home and later put a banister down the front steps going off the porch. Jeff put a banister on the steps going to the drive. It was important to make things safer for Harold, since he was growing more and more unsure of his balance.

Harold had ordered about five hundred white pine trees, but when they arrived he had the flu and was unable to get out of bed. So Jeff and I planted and planted. We also gave some to our neighbor. Quite a few of the trees did not live, I guess that is quite understandable.

Harold tried to come out and see to things but as a result he took a set back which turned into pneumonia. I finally got him to go to the doctor who gave him some antibiotics. However, instead of getting better, he got worse. When we went back to the doctor, he was so worried about the hardening of the arteries that he made an appointment for Harold at the University of Virginia.

But before his appointment, he got to the place where he could not breathe and we had to take him to the hospital. They were treating him for pneumonia, but the medicine was not doing him any good. They found out it was a rare kind of pneumonia and that behind the pneumonia were cancer spots. He was in the hospital three weeks that time. I would go with Brenda as she went to work, and stay all day, returning home at night.

After he came home, he never regained his strength. Still he wanted to keep busy, so he made a towel rack for the bathroom and put in up for me. We also got him a grandfather clock kit since he had always wanted one. He would get out of bed and work on it on the living room floor as long as he could stay up.

I know that Harold began to realize that he was dying, because he began to try to make things easier for me. He got me a new washer and had Tommy reline my wood stove with new fire brick. Harold also had Tommy and Jeff put new brake shoes on the Pinto, and made sure they put anti-freeze in it. He tried in every way to get things in order for me.

In between times, he was still going to church. We were going to Rockfish Valley Baptist church then. After we moved to Nelson County, we had visited three other churches, but Harold never seemed to settle down in any of them. Once a man had invited us to visit Rockfish Valley Baptist Church which was across the mountain from us and so we did. The pastor was an older man and Harold liked him. I felt led to join there, but waited to talk it over with Harold first. I had joined another church one day when he was sick and did not go and Harold was so upset because he did not want to go to that church.

Rev. Anderson from Rockfish Valley Baptist Church began to visit us. The first time he came, all the furniture was piled up in the living room floor because Tommy and Harold were working on the front door. I took Rev. Anderson and his wife to the kitchen to visit and we had sweet fellowship there. Harold came to really like him and they had many good conversations.

When I asked Harold about me joining the church, he said, "I think you would have to go a long way to find any nicer people."

From the very beginning the Lord began to give us a special love for those people. So I went forward, hoping he would follow me, but he did not.

Time passed, and Pastor and Antonette Anderson decided to leave Rockfish Valley Baptist Church. But just before they left, I felt led to invite him to dinner on a Saturday night.

Antonette was out of town. Chris was visiting me at the time and he said, "Grandma, Jeff and I have never been baptized." So, at the table I told Rev. Anderson about that. He looked at Jeff and said, "Jeff, are you ashamed of the Lord?" After talking to the boys for awhile, he looked at Harold and said, "Harold, when were you baptized?" Harold began to tell him about his Grandfather who was a Baptist preacher, and how his mother took him to church every Sunday. They talked about that for awhile, then went on to other things.

Later when Rev. Anderson started to leave, he asked Harold about his salvation. Harold said, "I would be afraid to walk the aisle at church." Rev. Anderson told him that he understood, because at one time he was afraid, too. That evening Rev. Anderson went home and changed his sermon. The next morning he preached on the five wise and the five foolish virgins, bringing out that we cannot depend on our parents, but each one of us is accountable before God. When the invitation was given, Harold was shaking all over. He said, "See what the boys are going to do."

That morning Jeff had been looking for something to wear to be baptized in, so I knew he was considering what to do. I said, "Jeff, are you going down?" He said, "I don't know." I said, "Jeff, get down that aisle." So down he went. Chris looked awhile and he went forward too. I went back to Harold and said, "Now what are you going to do?" He stood there a few minutes, I gave him a little shove and down he went. I felt such a sense of joy and victory that I sat and cried. Linda, a young lady in the church, came and put her arms around me. You would never doubt Harold's salvation if you could have seen him looking into Pastor Anderson's eyes and answering all his questions. I think he forgot anyone else was present.

That afternoon all three were baptized at Piney Mountain Bible Retreat in a branch of Rockfish River. Harold looked around and said, "This looks just like Fishing Creek where my Grandfather baptized." He had always said if he ever got baptized, he would like to be baptized in a place that looked like Fishing Creek. The retreat had been prepared that very week. Our church was the second one to use the creek for baptism.

The next day, I asked him how he felt and he said, "Just like the day after we were married. What have I gotten myself into now?" I think his statement expressed the conflict that many new Christians face between the old nature of the flesh and the new nature that Christ gives to us. He had been against the Christian faith for so long, I think he really feared what changes devotion to Christ would mean for him.

I remember telling my class again and again, that when the Lord gave me the assurance that Harold would be saved, we were living in Richmond, pastor Anderson was in Europe and we had never heard of Rockfish Valley Baptist Church or Piney Mountain Bible Retreat. And at God's appointed time He brought it all together. Not only did I have Harold's salvation, but two of my grandchildren's, too! Again the Lord did do exceedingly abundantly above all I could possibly ask or think. Praise His name!

When Antoinette got back, we were telling her about all that happened. Pastor Anderson said, "Yes, the Lord and Josephine's strong arm did it." I laughed and said, "You know as well as I, if that hadn't been of the Lord, it surely would have backfired on me."

Harold had to tell everyone about his baptism and how cold the water was. He was so happy that he had gone through with it.

Around this time my grandson, Eric, began to come to see us from time to time. We had not seen much of him since he was grown. It was so good to have him visit. Although he was not a believer, he would go to church out of respect for me. He was so thoughtful of his grandfather and we looked forward to his visits. I remember one of his visits especially. We were having Homecoming Day at church and Harold wanted to go so badly. So Kathy, Jeff's girlfriend, and I went ahead to make arrangements.

We took a lawn chair with pillows and a fan. The Sunday School teacher, Pete, moved her class outdoors so we could fix up a place for Harold. Since her classroom opened up to the sanctuary. Eric brought his grandpa and helped him get to his chair so he could hear the service. After the dinner, Eric took Harold home and let me stay for the afternoon meeting. When I got back home, Eric had to leave for Washington.

****

One day Harold wanted to go to the stock yards—of all places, to see what cows were bringing. So, I took him there. We stayed awhile and then I had to bring him home. That night Jeff and I had to take him to the hospital. When we got home at eleven o'clock that night, the neighbor called and said my cows had all been out on the highway. Her husband tried to get them, but could not. He did run them back in the woods. Well, there was nothing we could do then.

So, the next morning Jeff and I went out to look, but could not find them. I went back and fixed the fence where they had broken out. Jeff had to go to school because he was having a final exam. I remember coming in the house, so discouraged. I had a phone call to make, but before making it, I called out to the Lord to bring my cows back. When I finished my call and went out the door there stood my three cows by the back door!

I thanked the Lord and asked Him to help me get them back to the barn. I picked up a bucket and started to the barn. It had nothing in it, but the cows thought I was carrying food. As I started up the hill, not daring to look back, those three cows followed me like little puppy dogs. Then, they went in the gate, laid down, and slept all day.

I realized that something had to be done. Every time they would get out, I would be alone and would have to get someone to open the gate and hold it for me. So, I arranged that Saturday to have someone take them to the stock market. Jeff and I waited all day until they sold our cattle. Jeff was so proud that the check was in his name. Later that money was used to help bury Harold. John and Catherine, friends from our church, showed up and stayed all day with us. They bought us a cold drink and looked after us. They acted like they had just come to watch since John always sold his cattle there. They had heard that Jeff and I were going and he knew I did not know anything about cattle, so they really came to see that we got a fair deal. I will never forget that.

While Harold was in the hospital, a good friend of ours from the church died of cancer. She had been such a good Christian lady. She had entered the hospital just before Harold had to be readmitted. But the day before she had gone back into the hospital, she had taken a covered dish of food to another lady who also had cancer. In the midst of her pain and suffering, she was a shining example of Christ's love.

Since Harold was in the hospital when she went to be with the Lord, he wanted me to go on to her funeral. When I returned from the funeral, I could not find Harold in his room. When I inquired, they told me that he had fallen and struck his head.

When he got back from having x-rays done, he said, "Well, they put her in the ground didn't they?" By the way he talked, I knew that her death was troubling him. I know he felt some grief over her death. And I believe it also brought to mind that his own death was near.

When the doctor examined Harold, he was troubled by the disturbance in Harold's thinking. I followed him out of the room and told him about our friend, Faye, who had died. He was so relieved that I had told him. He said, "I was almost ready to tell Harold that he did not have long to live. I can see that would have been the wrong thing to do." Harold stayed in the hospital two weeks that time and then came home.

The summer of 1983 was the hottest and driest summer we had had in some years. Harold could not get his breath and we did not have air-conditioning. He had sold ours because he hated it.

Trying to make him confortable, we would move his cot to different areas of the yard, taking the fan with us. Finally, I had to clean the root cellar so we could put him in there when his breathing became difficult. One day, Keith, a friend of Harold's whom he had not seen in over forty years, called and said he heard that Harold was sick, and asked if he could come to see him. Well, Harold waited and waited. Finally he said, "I have to go to the root cellar. I can't breathe." He had no sooner gotten in there when Keith, and his wife and mother-in-law came. I told him that I was sorry but that if they wanted to see Harold they would have to go to the cellar. So they did. Later Marion and Blanche came up with me on the porch.

That day after they left, Keith called up some of Harold's friends. The following Sunday, they came down to put in a 220 line to the living room, and install an air conditioner that Keith had just taken out of his house. When Harold had trouble breathing, we turned on the air conditioner until he could breathe more easily. He still did not like it all the time, but at least he did not have to go back to the cellar.

Several months after Rev. Anderson had left Rockfish Valley Baptist Church, Steve and Teresa came. Harold knew that Steve, our new pastor, was just too young, twenty-seven years old, and he did not like him. But during Harold's illness, Steve was so compassionate. Through the months, Harold began to love him and lean on him. I know he grew to love Harold, too, and there was a oneness of spirit there.

I knew Harold did not have long to live, and I would think about what I would do when he was gone. One of my friends had lost her husband about two years before. Although she was a Christian, in seeking to overcome her loneliness she had turned from the Lord in the other direction. I did not want that to happen to me. Visiting church members and the unsaved came first after my love for the Lord Jesus, so I made a promise to the Lord that I would never put my housework before people.

By this time, Harold also knew that he was dying, but could not bring himself to talk about it. How much better it would have been if he could have faced his death openly and talked about his feelings and fears. I believe he had really wanted to talk to me about things in our past. On November 14, 1983, I took him back to the hospital. He was fighting for breath and I stayed with him that night. The next day, around eleven o'clock I came home for awhile and my grandaughter, Cathy, took my place.

I felt led to get a large ham on to cook, but I was so uneasy I had Jeff take me back to the hospital and bring Cathy home.

Steve, who had ministered to Harold over the past few months, came up and stayed until around nine. Harold told Pastor Steve that he hoped that he would soon get better so he could come back to church. Right after Steve left, Harold began to really have trouble breathing. Even though we had the fan on and he was under oxygen, he motioned for me to take a cardboard and fan him. I stood there from nine o'clock until two-thirty in the morning, fanning him. During this time a miracle happened. He opened his mouth and a flood of confession was released. He could not talk fast enough as he confessed to me all the wrong things he had done. Praise the Lord! Although I had left my hearing aid at home, the Lord let me catch just enough to know what he was talking about. I assured him that we loved him and wanted him to get well and come home. He wanted me to kiss him and I kissed him on the forehead. He just looked at me, as if he was searching my face to get a sense of my true feelings. To reassure him, I leaned over and kissed him on the mouth and he was satisfied. I think he knew that I had truly forgiven him.

And because he had repented and turned from all the wrong he had done, he knew too that God had forgiven him. What a blessed release that must have been!

Then, he looked up and the Lord in His tenderness gave him a vision. Harold kept looking and pointing his finger. He wanted me to see what he was seeing. Of couse, I could not see the vision. After that, he could not go on to be with the Lord soon enough. It seemed that he was literally trying to get out of the body. So much so, they said they had to tie him in bed to keep him from hurting himself. I told them I did not want that in my memories, so they let me lie down on the other side of the curtain. I could see his hand going back and forth, but drifted off to sleep about three a. m. At four they woke me up and said he was gone. He died on Novermber 16, 1983.

I know he really had wanted to express his sorrow over all the hurt between us, before now, but he did not have the courage. What relief he might have had and what sweet fellowship we could have had, had he done it sooner. But Praise the Lord, he made his peace before he died. I had an autopsy performed and there were five things that could have taken him at any moment.

They were amazed he lasted that long. There were seven years between the first bout of cancer and his death. I believe the Lord gave him the time so that he might have a real encounter with Jesus Christ. Our God longs for us to come to Him in faith, believing. We cannot fully understand the greatness and depth of

His love.

"The Lord is not slack concerning his promise, as some count slackness; but is longsuffering to usward, not willing that any should perish, but that all should come to repentance." II Peter 3:9

God does not send anyone to Hell. God has given unto us the way of salvation through faith in Jesus Christ. God gave His only Son to die on the cross so that we might be saved. It was a costly sacrifice. It grieved God to have Jesus Christ suffer and die on the cross. But God in Christ went all the way to the cross for us. And still He gives us the freedom to choose. And with that freedom comes the warning:

"How shall we escape, if we neglect so great salvation; which at the first began to be spoken by the Lord, and was confirmed unto us by them that hear Him;" Hebrews 2:3.

I am so thankful that Harold faced death with his hand in the hand of His Savior, Jesus Christ.

CHAPTER 21

Watching God Work

"Lo, children are the heritage of the Lord: and the fruit of the womb is His reward." Psalm 127:3

All the children came by when their daddy died. They began to make plans to make things easier for me. The boys arranged the funeral and no sooner was the funeral over than they all pitched in, children and grandchildren, to work things out for me. Some of them gave money and some came to work, some both.

Betty and Norbert were able to stay through Thanksgiving.

To help me around the house, they went upstairs and began to insulate and put up wallboard. When Norbert and family had to leave, Eric came and finished some of the work. I also was left with funeral and medical bills to pay. Harold did not believe in insurance, but I had a small policy. The boys helped me, by sending all the papers off and I managed to get all things together and pay off the funeral and some of the medical cost.

After Harold's death, I got back in church and took back my Sunday School Class. I wanted to start visiting, but I did not know where people lived in the community. Steve, our young pastor, had a similar desire. So we drifted to visiting together-always longing to win people to Christ. I loved teaching my class, and I loved visiting in their homes and getting to know them as friends. Harold and I had invited several of them to meals in our home and had come to know them better. Steve would set a time for visitation and announce it in the bulletin. I would be the only one to show up. So, we would go together.

One day, a lady told me that it was all over the Valley that I was running around with the pastor. I was certainly shocked, but I thanked her for telling me. I made it a matter of prayer for three days and that Sunday the Lord led me to go down in front of the church and tell what I had heard. Steve was about twenty-eight and I was seventy-seven. It seemed so ridiculous that anyone could think like that. Satan has tried in every way possible to discredit my testimony. Praise the Lord, "Greater is He that is in you than he that is in the world." (I John 4:4b)

The people of the church were shocked and they let us know that they knew it was not so. Still, I know someone had spread that rumor.

Satan works overtime to spread rumors and gossip and lies.

If he can keep a church torn apart, he is pleased. By going before the church and bringing it out in the open, I think it helped to put the fire of gossip out. I never heard anymore of it after that. I thank the Lord for Steve and Teresa because they stood with me during such times. Later they helped me during both of my automobile accidents. I have watched them grow so much in the Lord and I know God has a special purpose for their lives. Perhaps one day they will be on the mission field.

We have a wonderful Lord!

While teaching, I was led to tell how God had led me to get out of debt. It seemed that even though Harold had tried to get me prepared for handling the finances, so many things came up.

The only bill from the stores was for some pajamas I had ordered from Sears. Then my Pinto had to be inspected and I was going to have to get four new tires. I thought, "Well, I will go to Sears and get them and pay for them later." The Lord spoke to me, "What did you tell your Sunday School Class about getting out of debt?" So, I went home and cut up that credit card before I was tempted. I managed to get four recaps and got it inspected. So the Lord started me on the right track.

Larry, my son, had mentioned that if I had a certain amount taken out of my check and put in savings, I would have money for taxes, insurance, etc, without having to struggle when the bills came. This was another way the Lord led me. By following these principles, things have gone smoother. And I have not missed having a lot of money because I had never had much to spend.

In May of 1984, I was invited to go to Bryan College in Dayton, Tennessee for a Pastors' Seminar. I had always wanted to go to a place like that. Betty and Emmett, my friends from Richmond, were going and offered to take me. Emmett was the pastor at Winn's Baptist Church at that time. That April, I had a yard sale and got eighty dollars plus my Social Security check.

The Lord began to deal with me about the medical bills and

the grocery money I would need for my sister's visit at the middle of May.

Well, I laid it before the Lord. I had just enough in my savings to pay the medical bills. The trip to Bryan College would only cost me about thirty dollars since I would be riding with Betty. And I had enough for groceries. But in my heart, one Sunday, I was wondering what to do. I was out of gas and that Sunday they were taking a special offering to which I wanted to contribute. Lousie, my sister had already arrived from California. As she came down the stairs that morning, she had a ten dollar bill in her hand. She handed it to me and said, "This will help you on the gas." I thanked her. Then Eric who had come down for the week-end, offered me a twenty dollar bill.

As he gave it to me, he said, "This is for gas." When I told him that Louise had given me gas money, he said, "Well, give it to the church." I had not told either one of them about those two needs, but I knew that the Lord had answered my prayers that morning. It's such a life-changing feeling to know of God's real presence in your life.

That day after church, I had to tell them how God had answered my prayer. When Eric heard that and knew what my finances were, he went to the bank and put one hundred dollars in my checking account. So, I not only had a trip, paid off my medical bills, and had plenty of groceries, but I also finished the month of May with one hundred dollars in my checking account. I had a little plaque someone had given me which said, "Watch God work." Surely the last few years, that is what I have been doing. Praise His name!

When the children were together at the time of Harold's death, they had enjoyed seeing each other so much. So they made plans to come down in July to get together and get some things done for me. The first ones came the last of June and the last ones left August first. In July the highest number here at one time was thirty. It was a house full of family and fellowship and lots of work. After they had gone, I looked with great appreciation at all they had done. They had built a room for firewood on to the house. It matched the house, so that it could be made into a bedroom without too much expense. They installed an electric hot water heater. They placed a two-way light on the stairs next to the driveway which could be turned on at the front porch or at the driveway. They also built a small back porch, with stairs going up the hill and put a flood light to light up the back yard. There were crowds to feed but I still had money in my check book at the end of the month. Not only had they worked, but they had put their hands in their pockets to pay for things. How is that for watching God work?

He has surely blessed me through my family. They are so precious to me. They have shown so much love. Since then, from time to time different ones have come down and done things for me. Jeff lived with me then and kept the grass cut and did things around the house that I could not do. Several of my sons have bought me some beautiful dresses. I have nicer clothes now than I ever had.

I can remember years ago when Lottie went to town and bought me a beautiful coat. I loved that coat. It was so seldom that I ever got anything new that it really stood out. But all in all, I guess I have always had all that I needed. In I Timothy 6:6-8 Paul says, "But Godliness with contentment is great gain. For we brought nothing into this world, and it is certain we can carry nothing out. And having food and raiment let us be therewith content." By not having an abundance of material possessions in my life, I am truly thankful for the provision of my God through my family and friends. I truly know that my Creator and Redeemer cares for me. And I am so thankful for the care and love that my family has shown me.

CHAPTER 22

God Leads Us Along

"Lead me to the rock that is higher than I. For thou hath been a shelter for me, and a strong tower from the enemy." Psalm 61:2b-3

As I close this book, it is now the summer of 1986. It has been eight months since my accident in which I was trapped in my car for fourteen hours. I have regained my strength and I am looking to the Lord as to whether to start keeping my three grandchildren again. I feel He is leading in this way.

While I was visiting in Richmond the other day, I told Robin that I was writing this book. She said, "Oh, Grandma, be sure to put in that story you told about your sister and the warts. Everytime I look in the mirror and think how nice I look, I remember that story and quit looking in the mirror." This is the story I told my beautiful granddaughter, Robin when she was just a little girl:

When Margaret was dating, everyone would tell her how beautiful her lips were, so she would often go to the mirror and look at her lips. One day when she went to the mirror, her lips were full of little warts!

I am seventy-seven years old now. I have been a Christian since I was thirty-four years old. I thank God for the years he has given me to serve Him. There are so many stories that come to mind as I look back over my life.

I can remember Gertrude, my daughter-in-law, thinking I was silly for asking the Lord to help me find things. Then one day Bob, her little boy, took one of her silver knives out in to the yard and lost it. She looked everywhere for it and could not find it. The thought came to her mind that I always said the Lord helped me to find things. So feeling rather foolish, she asked the Lord to help her find it and walked right out the door right to it! She had to tell it in Sunday School that Sunday.

Lottie, who was in a home Bible study at the time, heard me say that I never set a clock because whenever I would tell the Lord what time I wanted to get up He would always wake me.

Before this, Lottie used several alarm clocks to wake her up.

So, she went home, turned off all her alarm clocks, and asked the Lord to wake her up. She really did not expect Him to wake her, but the Lord was leading her into a deeper walk, and to her amazement He did wake her up.

Glad, the precious one that led me to the Lord, always told me, "Whatever bothers you, tell the Lord about it. Nothing is too small to tell Him." I will always praise the Lord for leading her to me as she made my Lord real to me in everyday life. How much easier the going has been because I knew Him as a real person, not God afar off. He is ever near.

So many things I could say, so many experiences where precious ones were so good to me. I will never forget the wonderful times I had when we would go visit Opal. She always had her table loaded with food, and made everyone feel welcome.

Also, I have good memories of visits with my family.

There are many other things I could share, but above all I want this book to show forth the working of the Holy Spirit in my life. A couple of years ago, the Lord gave me these verses:

"Those that be planted in the house of the Lord shall flourish in the courts of our God. They shall still bring forth fruit in old age; they shall be fat and flourishing." Psalm 92:13-14

I thank God for the years He has given me and I humbly pray that I may continue to bear fruit for Him as Christ enables me.

The only purpose of this book is that the Lord and He alone be glorified. I pray that this book may help others to come to know my Savior and Lord Jesus Christ. I would hope that you know Him in a very real way as I have had the pleasure of knowing Him.

And as I am in the sunset of my life on this earth, I look forward to seeing my Savior face to face. As I began with this song, so shall I end:

"Away from the mire and away from the clay,
God leads His dear children along,
Away up in glory, eternity's day,

God leads His dear children along
Some thro' the waters, some thro' the flood,
Some thro' the fire; but all thro' the blood;
Some thro' great sorrow, but God gives a song,
In the night season and all the day long."
            G. A. Young

BIBLIOGRAPHY

Chapter 9
 Flint, Annie Johnson. "He Giveth More Grace". Poem No. 114. Faith, Prayer and Tract League. 2627 Elmridge Dr., N.W., Grand Rapids, Michigan. 49504-1390.*
 Tular, Grant Colfax. "The Weaver". Poem No. 53. Faith, Prayer and Tract League. 2627 Elmridge Dr., N.W., Grand Rapids, Michigan. 49504-1390.*

Chapter 14
 Sammis, John H. "When We Walk with the Lord". *Best Hymnal*. Nashville, Tennessee. Convention Press, 1975.

Chapter 17
 McConkey, James H. "Committal", 6-7. Richmond, Virginia. Silver Publishing, Braille Circulating Library.

Chapter 22
 Young, G. A. "God Leads Us Along".

All Scripture quotations are taken from the King James Version of the Bible unless indicated by N.I.V. which verses were taken from the New International Version of the Bible.

*Can be obtained in tract form.